PLANET HEARTBREAK

Other books by Vikki Stark

*Runaway Husbands: The Abandoned Wife's Guide
to Recovery and Renewal*

*The Divorce Talk: How to Tell the Kids
A Parent's Guide to Breaking the News
without Breaking Their Hearts*

*My Sister, My Self: The Surprising Ways That Being an Older,
Middle, Younger or Twin Shaped Your Life*

PLANET HEARTBREAK

Abandoned Wives Tell Their Stories

Edited by

Vikki Stark

Green Light Press

For information, contact:
Green Light Press
books@greenlight-press.com

Please visit: www.RunawayHusbands.com

Library and Archives Canada Cataloguing in Publication

    Planet heartbreak : abandoned wives tell their stories
/ Vikki Stark, editor.

Issued in print and electronic formats.

ISBN 978-0-9864721-8-3 (paperback).--ISBN 978-0-9864721-9-0 (PDF)

    1. Abandoned wives.   I. Stark, Vikki, editor

HQ805.P53 2016   306.88082   C2016-905024-6
                                           C2016-905025-4

Cover photo by Melanie DeFazio

*Dedicated to the 165 women who originally
submitted stories of their struggle to recover from
Wife Abandonment and to the countless other
women in our community who are fighting to love
life again.*

A friend of mine recently lost her husband to abandonment and she is devastated. In my journal, I wrote this: "I wish I could spare her the hours of crying, the self doubt, the bewilderment over how a man who swore he would be true to her forever could now hurt her like this, the feelings of being a non-person to him and all who worship him, of having to find her identity now that she is without him, of doubting even God's love for her – but I can't. She will have to work through those feelings herself, minute by minute, hour by hour, day by day, week by week, month by month. They are slow, long, and difficult but they do pass. With the help of friends and loved ones who listen and hold our hands, the healing of time comes and we women, brought so low by our men, rise again, stronger and better."

Marcela from San Antonio, Texas

Contents

Introduction

Ten years ago my husband left. There was not the slightest whiff in the air to alert me that the weather in my life was about to change. I, like you perhaps, believed from the bottom of my heart that he was as invested in the marriage as I was. I was devastated when he left.

I suffered profoundly and grappled with many of the same problems you are struggling with. I desperately needed to understand how this Mack truck of destruction could suddenly materialize out of nowhere. How could someone I thought I knew to the core of his being actually be so very different? How could the marriage just slip through my fingers? How do I contact him again to talk to the old him—the one who loved me and cared so much . . . or so I thought? And had he really loved me? If he did, how could he sneak away so calculatedly, like a thief in the night, taking my life as I knew it? How could he then turn against me?

How could the person I trusted most in the world, betray me?

I'm a marriage counselor so when my husband left, I scoured the literature looking for answers and found almost none. I started to realize that I was not the only woman to whom this had happened. I needed to know more so I conducted a world-wide study called the Sudden Wife Abandonment Project (SWAP—like he swapped me for the other woman). I interviewed four hundred women worldwide and the results were breathtaking.

I was able to map out a very defined set of behaviors consistent among the husbands who left out-of-the-blue from what their wives believed to be stable, committed, or even happy marriages. It was shocking to hear the eerily identical stories in detail from women in far-flung cultures all over the world.

As a result, I wrote the book *Runaway Husbands: The Abandoned Wife's Guide to Recovery and Renewal,* which became a game changer in my life and, I've been told, in the lives of a multitude of devastated women, left alone and looking for answers. Many women have told me they devoured the book and finally felt such relief, understanding what happened to them, knowing they are not crazy, not alone and not to blame. They read it and re-read it and even carry it around with them in their purse.

In writing *Runaway Husbands,* I shared with my readers my own experience of wife abandonment and everything I subsequently learned as a result. I explain how and why a man can morph overnight from a loving husband to an angry stranger. I provide women with tools to get relief from the emotional pain, obsessive thoughts and profound grief. I help readers track their step-by-step recovery through the "Transformational Stages." I offer vignettes from the stories of the women who participated in SWAP so that readers will know they are not alone.

From the book, *Runaway Husbands,* grew the website, *runawayhusbands.com,* which has been visited by hundreds of thousands of women from every single country in the world. Women who, in the middle of a sleepless night, tearfully typed "wife abandonment" or "my husband left" into Google and found themselves a home with us—members of a tribe we never wanted to join.

To help break the sense of isolation, I began *Healing Circles,* in which I introduce women to others who live in the same town or area. Sometimes it clicks and they form their own self-directed local support group. There are *Healing Circles* functioning all over the world! Some groups have many women; some, just two who have become close friends and comrades.

I've conducted *Healing Circles* on-line. We meet for eight sessions at a specific time and discuss our lives and how to heal from Wife Abandonment Syndrome. It's amazing to have a close group of friends made up of women from Australia, Europe, the United States and Canada providing support for each other. When someone's dog barks in Australia, someone else's dog hears it through the computer and responds from California. It's crazy!

The initiative that literally brings us together is the retreats that I hold in Montreal (two days) and in Sedona, Arizona (four days). I can't tell you how meaningful it is to me to meet "my girls" face-to-face and see how much healing and growth happens when women get together. Everyone takes a leap forward following a retreat, finally understanding what happened, remembering who she is, and getting a glimpse of who she can be!

It's a noble tribe, populated with some pretty special women—women like you! Women who have suffered and struggled to regain dignity in spite of everything they are going through, women who have learned about life and how to overcome suffering, sometimes even using it as a springboard for change.

That's where *Planet Heartbreak* comes in. The book you are about to read will take you on a healing journey. You will learn how sixty-two other women grappled with and solved, or are still struggling to solve, the same things you're dealing with in your life. You will read stories that mirror your own to a tee and that will help you. And you will feel the raw humanity of the writers who reach out to you with their advice and encouragement. We're all in this together—all part of this tribe at varying points along the same journey. Please know that I'm walking with you, as are all the other Runaway Husbands wives.

HOW TO READ *PLANET HEARTBREAK*

Planet Heartbreak is a companion volume to *Runaway Husbands: The Abandoned Wife's Guide to Recovery and Renewal*. You will get the most out of it if you've already read *Runaway Husbands*.

The sixty-two stories are in no particular order. They are identified by the name of the contributor, her age, her location, and how long since the separation took place. I did not include the length of time since an actual divorce took place—some of the women are divorced and some not.

The contributors were given the option to identify themselves using their real name or provide an alias. You will not know which stories carry the writer's true identity. The age and length of time since separation are true in all cases.

It was important to me to preserve the mood and intention of each story so, for example, stories written by Brits, Australians and Canadians keep British spelling (flavour instead of flavor). Some stories are filled with raw emotion – lots of CAPS and exclamation points!!! I wanted you to feel what the writer was trying to express so I kept all that in.

Planet Heartbreak is not an easy read but I'm hoping that, like listening to a sad song, it mirrors your reality and comforts you. It can be profoundly healing to hear your own song sung by someone who really understands how you feel.

You may only be able to spend short bursts of time with the book. You may have to read several stories to locate the ones that really resonate. Many of the stories start off the same, but keep reading. Inside each you'll find a nugget of wisdom, a flash of beauty, a bell of truth or a twist. My deepest wish is that this book soothes your pain and helps you know, really know, that you are not alone. There are lots of us on Planet Heartbreak.

Vikki Stark, Editor
Author of *Runaway Husbands: The Abandoned Wife's Guide to Recovery and Renewal*

1

Abandonment 101: How to Keep Your Sense of Humour when Your World Is Turned Upside Down

Judith from Alberta, Canada
58 years old
Separated nine years

"I have no drive or desire to continue in the marriage." The words stung and shocked, made even more painful by the fact that they were the opening line of an e-mail, sent to me in the summer of 2007 by my husband of twenty-two years while I was out of town visiting a friend. A split second was all it took for the world as I knew it to forever change, and for the man I deeply loved to become a stranger.

In that bolt-from-the-blue moment, I thought I had perhaps hacked into someone else's e-mail account, but that was virtually impossible. I barely knew how to work my new smartphone, let alone become a cyber threat. Like many other women who have been suddenly abandoned, I had no idea my marriage was in trouble, let alone over. Attempts to communicate with him about what was happening were futile; he was distant, emotionless, gone.

His behaviour was also baffling and bizarre. He didn't understand why I had a problem with him living in the basement for two years. "Like a troll?" I asked, incredulous at his idiocy. His last words to me before he packed a few belongings and left forever were, "I expect to be crucified."

He got what he expected. For the next five years, the legal battle raged on, he with his high-priced lawyer from another city, and I unrepresented not by choice but by circumstance. I wanted to keep a roof over my head, not put a new one on some lawyer's mansion.

It wasn't easy. I had no legal training or background, just my intelligence, my communication skills as a writer, and a newly discovered set of Lady Balls that made his look like walnuts. Small walnuts. I firmly believed I had nothing more to lose—I had no job and no marriage, I was an empty-nester, and both my parents were elderly and fragile. I was fighting for my future, at all cost.

But there were other costs, far more scarring than the legal and financial ones, and longer lasting. For the first two years at least, I was profoundly destabilized and depressed. I was hospitalized. I was prescribed antidepressants and sleeping medication, and I began having panic attacks. I had nightmares every night for years. I never had another period after he left, and I wasn't in the menopausal age group. I isolated myself from family and friends as I grappled to make sense of the deep shame I felt. My thought process was skewed: *What kind of woman gets abandoned?* rather than *What kind of man abandons his wife?*

I struggled with trying to understand why my children would want to have any kind of relationship with the person who had so cruelly hurt their mother. I was so lost in my own pain and suffering that I did not know of their anguish at suddenly being from a "broken family" and feeling torn. I did not make it easy for them and I made a lot of mistakes. It was a bleak time.

In my self-imposed isolation, I ruminated and agonized over questions I would never get answers for: *Why hadn't I seen this coming? Had my marriage been a complete lie? Did he ever really love me?* And most of all, *How was I going to get over this and ever truly and fully Let Go?* I was numb and impervious to the notion that any peace could come from this.

As I began to spend the equivalent of a full-time job researching case law, spousal support guidelines, and how to dispose of certain items without getting caught (OK, just kidding . . . sort of), the emotional divorce took a back seat. As I studied book after book on divorce, easily a dozen or more, and prowled the Internet for process and procedure, I learned that The Law doesn't really care whether the ex was a passive-aggressive coward with daddy issues. The Law only cares about The Law and what is supported by The Law. I created a separate binder for The Emotional Divorce and filed anything and everything in there that had to do with feelings.

Because I experienced physical symptoms of anxiety if I used his name (think retching sounds), I began to refer to him simply as the X. One letter only, no need to waste any more of the alphabet. I depersonalized and de-gendered "that person" as much as possible, finding it difficult to use the word "man"; real men may not eat quiche, but real men don't throw their wives to the curb like trash. In my legal documents, he was always "your client" or "the defendant."

By December of 2012, over five years from the day I received that life-altering email, the "Crucifixion" was complete and I had won the Divorce Wars. I was awarded everything that I had fought so long and hard for, and then some. A lawyer friend asked, "How did you manage to get this settlement? I certainly couldn't have got this for you. It must have been his guilt." I had no answer. All I felt was relief and an ever increasing emotion that was completely bewildering to me. Anger.

After all I had been through and all I had accomplished, I was overwhelmed with anger. I struggled to understand where the anger was coming from, but it made no sense at all. During an outing to a gala event with my daughter, the X showed up with his Next Wife. Even though I live in a fairly small city, I had been blessed with only running into the X on a handful of occasions over the years. Seeing him made me feel physically ill and, as the wine flowed a little too freely, I semi-hatched a plan to creep up behind him and whack him over the head. Luckily, my daughter caught wind of my foolish plan and escorted me from the premises.

I realized I needed some help to sort out what I was going through (and stay out of jail!), so I contacted a woman who worked with people who had been traumatized. I didn't have much faith that she could help me, but I had tried just about everything else and was desperate to stop feeling the way I did.

What I learned put me on the path to healing. Not only had I been severely traumatized by the abandonment, I had become stuck. Instead of "fight or flight," I had been frozen for a long time. I learned that as I came out of this frozen state, it was not uncommon that one of the first emotions to emerge was anger. I learned techniques to cope with my anxiety and anger, and looked for other ways to continue to heal the past, and finally to Let Go.

I attended my first retreat with Vikki Stark in Sedona, Arizona, in the fall of 2013. I was ready and able to receive comfort and healing along with a small group of beautiful but broken women who had all walked in my shoes. We cried, we laughed, we bonded, we cried and laughed some more. We remain in touch to this day. I wound up doing a stand-up comedy routine the following year in Montreal at another of Vikki's retreats. It was heartwarming and soul affirming to hear the uninhibited laughter from a group of women who had just joined the Abandoned Wives Club and didn't know what to do with their membership card that they'd just as soon burn.

If you find yourself as a newly inducted member of the AWC, or on the executive committee because of your long years of service, please know that there will come a day when the X can no longer hurt you. You will be free. You will grow and learn and love and be loved. You are not alone. Those of us who have been to hell and back and reinvented ourselves in ways we couldn't have imagined way-back-when are here to guide and support you as you heal the past, live the present, and dream of a magnificent future.

2

So It Hit Me

Debbie from Sechelt, British Columbia, Canada
57 years old
Separated eleven months

So it hit me. Square in the face. That burst of heat flashing your skin as you absentmindedly open the oven door. Intense and instant—bringing you to your senses. The blindsiding words, "I don't love you anymore. I want a divorce." In a flash, flesh-searing pain and the ripping of the heart. The primal scream of death.

And so it was on that Sunday afternoon. Ten days in a car with his two sisters, a road trip to visit my new granddaughter and a couple of thousand miles. He stayed home. Bad back he said. Have fun with the girls. And when I returned that Sunday afternoon I walked into the kitchen and blindly opened the oven door.

No I missed you hugs. No "Wait till you hear the stories." Only an empty silence and a feeling of, "What the hell is going on?" And then those crippling words—"I want a divorce." No need to talk or see a counsellor. Just the chalk-screeching reality that he had made up his mind and I had no say in the matter. He had given this a lot of thought, he said. He had taken care of everything. There was a lawyer for him. A lawyer for me. The bank account had been divided, the credit card cut off, real estate agent consulted, and immediate family informed. The beneficiary of the Divorcing Debbie Club was the last to know. Bam! Blindside! Tossed right into the oven!

And so I sit, five decades plus six years facing a future on my own. The teenage sweethearts had defied the odds for forty-one years but now the gig was over. We had grown together as one soul, not as two individuals, melded together for eternity. Now I needed to learn to live as one when my very breath had been taken away along with half my body and my heart. At this stage, how could I re-invent myself when for so long we were one entity cooking in life's kitchen? Should I turn off the electric range? Switch to gas? Stop cooking . . . or get out of the kitchen all together?

But what I really wanted to do was to re-enter the kitchen facing a different scenario. I wanted to run into his strong arms, feel the warmth of his skin, and share the trials and triumphs of travelling with the in-laws. I wanted to tell him our granddaughter was a delight and healthy and happy. I wanted to tell him of the personal epiphanies that enlightened me during endless hours of highway travel. Oh, how I would give anything to walk through that door and smell fresh bread, knowing the oven was already cooling.

But reality had produced its own recipe. Take two lawyers, add countless dollars, file many forms, and sprinkle with tears. Yield two single people no longer attached by commitment to live together until death do us part. One not ready for the mixing bowl and the other already on the cooling rack.

Phone calls needed to be made. Relatives informed. Living arrangements procured interspersed with hysterical conversations wrought with anger, disbelief and, yes, some foul language. Hurtful things. Bitter words. Raw emotion. He was cold and calculating, having had time to already process and rehearse the scene playing out. Nonchalant and cool. Oh—and by the way—how was the trip? Are you kidding me? And just like that, the oven door slammed shut forever. And it was over. I was totally and irreversibly and utterly alone.

The house is big. It is new and full of light and colour. Peaceful forest can be seen from every window, with peek-a-boo views of the distant ocean. But today a forest fire is lurking. The sky is casting an eerie yellow glow on the world below. The air is filled with acrid smoke, and ash flitters through the air like campfire snowflakes caught on the breeze. How appropriate for this ominous moment—even Mother Nature has left her cookies in the oven for too long.

And I am alone to sift through the ashes of my whole world and question the meaning of my existence. Tears flow enough to extinguish the 150-hectare fire. I cannot think. I cannot move. I cannot eat or drink. I stare at the ceiling and wish for the winds to blow the ravaging fire directly into my path. I cannot sleep. I am alone with forty-one years of ifs and buts and how I could have written a different recipe. But none of this matters anymore. He has made his decision. It is his final answer.

The sound of his car jolts me out of my reverie. He is home to water the garden. I get off the couch, trailing my comforter behind me and stare out the window as his car backs away. He spots me as it turns. Then stops and timidly waves. I am not sure what I see in his eyes. I hope a little sadness. Tears flood my view but my fingers wave back in sorrow. He has not yet really said good-bye. I am ambushed by heart-wrenching sobs. His car rolls down the driveway and out of sight. As day two dawns, I stumble downstairs to the smoke-filled skies reminding me that everything is still aflame. The trees. The grass. My heart. I wrap myself in the family cozy blanket and stare mindlessly out the window. Tomorrow I must return to work. A task I am not yet prepared to face.

But before work, one more call to make. My oldest child has been on an epic journey of her own, hiking a trail and out of verbal contact for over two months. Today she has arranged to call, anxious for an update on the family turmoil. While sad at the breakup of the family, she reminds me to rejoice in the happy memories. They don't cease to exist because the marriage is over. She wisely reminds me that this is time to look after myself. To grieve, to cry, but always with the intent that better days are ahead. She echoes the sage advice of many friends that this is not the end but the beginning of something new and exciting. And I will survive and be stronger and more fulfilled in the end. But please don't cut Dad out of the family photos. They are still her memories. Our family memories.

And then it begins. I approach the oven timidly and give it a glance. A quick glance, mind you, but nonetheless a glance. And I see before my eyes the opportunities I am afforded living my life alone. The chance to share in the lives of my grandchildren without any hidden guilt. The chance to travel wherever the urge takes me. To eat whatever I choose without the guardian of the calories watching over my shoulder. And to make microwave popcorn on a whim.

But the closeness of the oven reminds me I will always return to an empty kitchen. No one to tell the stories to. Something is lost when you have no one to share these moments. So . . . how was my trip with my sisters-in-law? Quite honestly, I have forgotten. The excitement of wanting to share the travel tales with him has been eaten up by the shadow of divorce. And so it goes. One small step. One small glance. With the assurance of my young and wise sages, I know that in time, I will be back in the kitchen and cooking with fire!

3

Still Standing

Julie from Worcester County, Massachusetts, USA
52 years old
Separated eight years

My story began around Thanksgiving 2007. After returning from a business trip in the UK my husband told me he wasn't happy, that he loved me but wasn't in love with me, and that he needed space. I remember that moment like it was yesterday, complete shock. The world stood still, my ears buzzed, and I went totally numb. The word "devastation" doesn't adequately describe the pain I felt then and going forward; it was crippling and all-encompassing. From that moment on he became a totally different person, one who dragged us all on a journey that can best be described as an excellent storyline for a soap opera and would be totally entertaining except that this story was real and was happening to me.

We had been together for thirty years and married for almost twenty. We immigrated to America in 1993, with an infant son in tow so that my husband could further his career. I was a midwife who had supported him throughout school; he was a recent PhD graduate. It was hard, but we were young. We were a team, and leaving my country, family, and career was an adventure! After all, we were building our lives and an awesome future. We had a daughter and life was good. I never once believed I had married the wrong person. He was kind and affectionate, we still held hands, he wrote beautiful cards, and those who saw how we interacted felt that we had something special.

I had heard all the infidelity stories and always thought, *Oh, she must have known!* But you don't. Fooled by complete trust and having been cocooned in a life where I had never been "majorly" lied to, I missed it.

He ended up leaving in March of 2008, and the typical clichéd script started. "There is no other woman," "I have been unhappy for years," "You got fat," "You are never happy," "You are not normal," "You are a psycho," "You are too controlling," "You spend too much," and my favorite, "I just want the easy life." Over the next few months the truth unfolded.

The reality. He was a middle-aged vice president of a biotech company who had gotten involved with a co-worker soon after he employed her, a woman fifteen years younger who had only been married nine months herself. No doubt the fact that he was successful with a high salary and had a cute British accent was the lure for her. In the preceding few years, his father had passed away and our son was diagnosed with a form of OCD. The perfect storm for infidelity I have since learned.

Eight years later this is what I have learned.

You will be made to feel worthless. This level of betrayal does that. You are normal. You will lose your way and it will be hard to function. Keep standing. You will distrust your intuition and your internal compass will be thrown. Have faith. You will be told everything is your fault. Don't believe it. Most of the time a runaway husband will not take responsibility for his own actions. Even faced with overwhelming evidence, mine still denied any wrongdoing and hurled all manner of accusations at me in order to justify his behavior.

Stay strong and know he is just following a well-documented script, one in which history is rewritten, denial is rife, and blame is projected and assigned to you. You are not crazy or psychotic, and you did not imagine your life with him. This is an ego-protective defense mechanism, one that is deployed so that the ex-spouse doesn't have to feel the pain of his actions. They box themselves off, build a new reality, and surround themselves only with those who feed it.

Your life will be levelled and he will not care. You will think you will not get through it, but you will. Keep standing. Your life has just been spring cleaned, and here is the gift (although you will not see it at the time)—you get to rebuild it! You get to choose what stays in it and what you discard. Comfort and surround yourself with things you love.

I remember a quote from William Morris, which seemed poignant at the time: "Have nothing in your house that you do not know to be useful, or believe to be beautiful." Being in a crisis gives you the perfect excuse to politely remove all those toxic people and things that you only tolerated in your life previously. There is a freedom here, a chance to prune the dead wood and focus with laser sharpness on only what is important.

The guy who you previously knew to be kind and loving will become vicious and cruel. When things don't go his way in court, especially in all matters financial, he will become angry and irrational. He will punish and withhold. In my case he refused all communication and returned all mail, forcing trips to court for contempt. I have had police at my door because he claimed I was abusing the children and summons to court because he claimed I was harassing him. Throughout it all, even though my resolve wavered, I knew in my heart of hearts how wrong this all was. The more resolute I became and the straighter I stood up, the angrier he became. There were times when his behavior became so irrational that I felt like I had just entered Crazy Town.

Give yourself time to grieve, seek counseling, surround yourself with loving friends and family, and read all the literature you can. This is your journey and healing is on your timetable, no one else's. My healing was hampered by well-meaning people who believed I should have moved on earlier than I did. I had to deal with thirty years of memories that every day would be triggered by a song, a smell, a place. It will happen, it will be unexpected, you will cry, but it will lessen. The pain is real. Being amputated from a life is beyond traumatic, but it is important to walk through every bit of it.

To this day we still have no answers, and closure has been in the form of a lidless box, not packaged up nice and pretty but rather cobbled together as best I could. My ex did end up getting the new woman pregnant. They have subsequently got married and had another child, so we heard. We are not in contact; the kids have never met them, and they have not heard from him in four years. For the children, the hardest part has been his abandonment and his refusal to admit that he did anything wrong. The saddest part is that he has two beautiful kids whose pain has gone unacknowledged and who now feel replaced and displaced. The new woman and family were always put first, graduations were not attended because she was not invited, and emotional support has been withheld because they refuse to accept her.

There are still times when I am in total disbelief about what we went through. But we survived, we are strong, we are whole, and we are still standing.

4

If Life Gives You Lemons, Make Lemonade

Susan from Wales, UK
62 years old
Separated two years

My husband and I were together for forty years. We went through a lot together, mainly his three life-threatening illnesses. I worked full time and brought in a good wage; he went onto benefits but was capable of working.

We weren't an overtly affectionate couple, but I thought we would always love each other. We liked the same music, films, theatre, TV programmes—I thought we were "in tune."

He arranged an expensive cruise for us, but on the day after we got back, he said he was going to meet a friend for coffee. He was out of contact all day. I texted my son asking if he'd seen his Dad. My (ex now) husband came home at nine that evening, started making a meal for us, and said, "I am leaving you."

He wanted to live with a woman twenty-five years younger who has no children and never had a proper job. He had a financial plan already devised whereby he would take a lot of money. He had told everyone, including my children, that he was going to leave me when we got back from the cruise. I was blissfully ignorant.

I was so surprised and devastated, I hugged him and told him it would all be OK. You see, I love him enough not to want to cause him any stress because of his heart problems. Also, I could see that he really loves this young woman, who is the same age as my son and two years older than my daughter.

She says he is her "oxygen," she can't breathe without him. She wants to be with him 24–7. He said he wanted to wake up every day and everything to be about him. I couldn't do that because I give time to my kids and grandkids—my fault for not prioritising him.

So, I did not contest the divorce, in which he blamed me for his having to leave. He came back three times but realised he no longer loved me and wanted to be with her.

I realised that I couldn't make him love me anymore, so I apologised to him and asked for forgiveness for not being the wife he needed, let him take whatever he wanted, and took all the blame. He had repeatedly told me to change during our marriage, but I buried my head in the sand and carried on in my own way, being busy with work, family, friends, and hobbies. He obviously felt that he wasn't needed. She makes him feel that he is awesome. I am pleased for him, that he has found his soul mate.

I have filled my life. I have returned to working two days a week (after retiring), to a job I have always loved, helping children with additional needs. I volunteer with four different wildlife conservation groups—being outdoors with nature and lovely people has saved me—so good for the soul. I have joined an amateur dramatics group as a stagehand and props maker. I go to exercise classes.

In fact, I am never in the house, because that is when I fall apart. I am lonely; I miss him, and constantly think of them together—my "husband" telling another woman that he loves her and all that entails. I am moving on slowly with a life I never envisaged, but I have no choice. I have bad days and not so bad days (not many good days yet), but I am surviving. I am grateful that I am fit and healthy for my age and that I have my family. (Although that is now broken—my son and daughter are not on good terms because of this; she is less forgiving of her dad because her ex fiancé did the same thing to her).

I have a house, enough money to pay the bills, friends, and hob-bies. I keep telling myself that there are so many people with worse lives than mine. I have had counselling, which helped a little. I have learned a lot about myself and have become a better person—a lis-tener, empathic and compassionate—all the things he said that I wasn't. I do yoga, meditation, and mindfulness. I'm proud that I can fix things for myself around the house, and I can sort out all the finan-cial aspects that he always dealt with.

All I hope for is that he is happy. I still love him and want that for him. I don't blame him because you can't help who you fall in love with. I may eventually meet someone else (although I am not hopeful at 62 years of age), but I would make sure that any new man in my life felt appreciated and needed.

For now, I have to love myself, forgive myself for my perceived flaws and mistakes, take care of myself physically and emotionally, and wait for the time when I no longer feel hurt and abandoned. In my head I know that this time will come; I am just waiting for my heart to catch up.

This is what we must believe and trust to happen. Get through each day and the days will become weeks, months, and years, and we will survive. If life gives you lemons, make lemonade.

5

Life Is Not a Dress Rehearsal

Kathleen from Florida, USA
69 years old
Separated five years

I married in 1969 at the age of 21. My divorce was final forty-three years later. On June 10, 2012, on a plane returning from New York City, where I had been babysitting my first infant grandson, I realized that my "wasbund" had inadvertently left his phone on after confirming with me that the flight was on time. I sat on a darkened airplane listening to him talking about me with my former best friend of twenty-one years. It was a conversation that left no doubt that he had been having an affair with her for nearly five years.

Foolish me—it was a repeat for him, as he had been caught once before by this woman's husband. After he had pleaded to return and swore that he only loved me, I had taken him back and trusted that it had just been an indiscretion.

He and I were close friends, shared everything with each other, took fantastic bike trips all over the world, and were intimate. It was not a perfect marriage but seemed to me to be stronger and more transparent after his affair with this close family friend. My adult daughters, my mother, my family and our friends forgave him. A bump in the road of a very long marriage . . . or so I thought.

So, I was beyond devastated when I heard her voice and their conversation on that fateful plane ride. It was as if my world had shattered. My very strong ego and ample self-esteem evaporated. It was as if I had fallen into a dark hole and couldn't find any escape. It was a very tough time for me; I lost thirteen pounds in two weeks, became suicidal at one point, cried continuously, and then I simply snapped out of it. Determination, rage, fear—not sure what it was, but I refused to give in to my depression.

Fortunately today—nearly five years later—my life is better than I could have ever imagined. I realize now in hindsight that there was an insidious benign neglect on his part that I had failed to see, and it had been eating away at me for years. Today I love my independence, my women friends, renewed spirituality, sobriety (four days after that plane ride I had my last drink!), and a wonderful male partner. I have travelled around the world (including three very long-distance bike trips), bought a car all by myself, become a regular at Home Depot, learned how to meditate, and I have a close relationship with my daughters and four grandsons.

How did I do it? I picked myself up and vowed that "he" would not ruin my life and that a life well lived was the only revenge worth seeking. In many ways I feel sorry for him. He is a grumpy, old man with few friends and a very tenuous relationship with our kids and grandkids. Life is not a "dress rehearsal," so it is crucial to work at getting better. It doesn't happen without work and commitment. Personal growth is enormously rewarding, and crisis opens the door to that growth. So each day I treasure challenges as a way to further my journey in life and feel blessed to have had the opportunity to find the path I am on.

Learning to Live with
What's Left of My Grief

Anna from Viborg, Denmark
42 years old
Separated one year

We had both had a busy day, and I was blathering about mine when he interrupted me and said, "We need to talk." I instantly understood something really bad was coming up, but I had no idea of the magnitude of what was going to happen.

He wanted a divorce. "I can't go on this way," he explained. "Please begin to consider whether you want to move out or stay in the house, and what kind of arrangement you want with the kids," he went on saying. Needless to say, I was in shock. "Are you in love with another woman?" I asked him mechanically. He shook his head in denial.

Fourteen months prior to that evening, we had bought the house of our dreams—the house where our three kids would grow up, the house where we would get old together. One and a half months prior to that evening, we had been out looking for a new car. A couple of weeks prior to that evening I woke up in tears in the middle of the night. "I dreamt that you left me for another woman," I sobbed. "There is no other woman," he said, and took me lovingly in his arms.

For the next several weeks I was totally numb. I woke up in the morning and cried, got into the car and drove to work, came back and began to cry again. "She misses her mum," my husband explained to the kids. He didn't want me to tell the kids right away. He wanted to wait until one of us moved out. Also, he wanted to tell the kids it was a decision we both had agreed on.

When we finally told the kids, they were in shock too. Yes, we had had some rough spots as a couple, but that was years and years ago, when the kids were little. Besides, which couple doesn't have rough spots in their marriage?

I cried for days. "How can you stare at me crying and do nothing? You're not a human being, you are a monster!" I burst out one evening. "Yes, and it's all your fault. You made me into the monster I am today," he replied coldly. And indeed, what was killing me was his distant attitude, his being completely and utterly indifferent about the whole situation. And, of course, his blaming me for the whole situation.

Two weeks after he told me he wanted a divorce, I found out I was pregnant with our fourth child. He got in a rage when I told him.

My family and friends kept saying there must be another woman. A 40-year-old man doesn't walk out on his wife of seventeen years unless he has found another. But he kept denying that until I forced him to admit it. He would have told me and the kids after one year, he said. It was a co-worker—one he had met some months before. I'd had no idea. My husband, whom I trusted more than anyone else in the world, had been faking and lying for months, "for years actually," as he once put it, being married to a woman he no longer loved.

Today I am the single mom of four kids. Am I happy? Kind of. I still despise my children's father, but I try to look at what happened as a possibility to grow as a person and as a parent. Although I still feel very lonely, I do not want a partner at this point in time. Do I understand what happened? No, and I still think what happened is unbelievable. Will I ever forgive him? Well, you can't really forgive somebody who doesn't think he has done something wrong. But I try to accept—not understand—what happened and to be kind to myself for my own sake and peace of mind.

Reading *Runaway Husbands* truly saved me from going insane. Instead of blaming it all on me, I now keep saying to myself that no matter how bad I might have been as a wife, I did not deserve to be treated the way he treated me.

Time is a huge factor in the healing process too. It's been a year now, and although I can't say I am over it, I am learning to live with what's left of my grief. It's been awful, and I'm still in the turmoil of my feelings, but it's very slowly getting better. There are no real shortcuts here, I'm afraid.

💔

Love Is an Action Word

Stevia from Chicago, Illinois, USA
52 years old
Separated one year

We had only been married one year when my husband mentally, emotionally, and spiritually left our marriage. Sure, we had arguments, but all couples argue. I've thought about the "why" of it all so often, I mean, how everything seemed to just fell apart. We were in ministry together. People's lives were being changed, but ours had fallen apart. I loved my husband and I thought he loved me too.

"You have thirty days to get your stuff and get out. I'm moving out of state." He said this in a phone call, five minutes after he'd left the house! I was blindsided and in complete and utter shock.

"Huh? What do you mean? Isn't this something we need to talk about?"

"No, there isn't anything left to talk about. I'm done and our marriage is over."

"But . . . wait a minute what's going o . . ."

He'd cut me off in mid-sentence. "I said there's nothing to talk about." Click. He'd hung up.

I sat at the breakfast table trying to finish my breakfast. I couldn't. I couldn't believe this was happening! My stomach and chest began to hurt. Where would I go? How would I support myself? Why was this happening!? After a couple of hours I called my dad and asked if I could stay with him while I got on my feet. He was shocked. "What do you mean? I don't understand." The tears began to flow, and I couldn't get a coherent sentence out. "Sure you can come and stay with me. You have the key. I'll see you in a few minutes."

When I got to my dad's house I was numb, ashamed, and extremely angry. While I was racing around our apartment like a banshee trying to gather my belongings, I was running on autopilot and sheer adrenaline. I wnet through each room, determining what I could take, what I could move by myself, what I wanted to leave behind that might remind me of this horrible man I'd given my life to. On top of all of this, I didn't know if and or when he was coming back. I just wanted to be gone before he did.

Our neighbors across the hall had just gotten married and we'd invited them to our Bible study. What were they thinking, seeing me move my items out of our apartment? On one of my many trips to unload my car at my dad's one-bedroom apartment, I saw a mutual friend. I was so embarrassed. She knew something was going on by the dried tears and look of sadness on my face. She knew my husband and I were in ministry, and she knew he wasn't helping me move our items into a new apartment. She lived in the same building as my dad and saw me and my husband moving my things out to our new place in the next building over when we were first married. I couldn't even talk to her.

My body was aching, my mind was reeling, and my heart was broken. All I could think of during the many trips of loading and unloading my car was that I was being rejected. (I'd been rejected so many times by my mother.) I had been lied to. How was God going to help me get through this? I cried myself to sleep every night and forbade my dad to say the enemy's (my husband's) name.

Finally, as the adrenaline began to wear off and the days passed and I'd begun to settle into my new life in the half of living room and sleeper sofa that was to be my life, the bitterness and perpetual anger grew exponentially and were my constant companions. I'd come from a spacious two-bedroom apartment to this! The thoughts *He couldn't even talk to me face to face! He had to leave the house, then call me to tell me to leave! Coward! Loser! Some man of God you are!* kept replaying in my mind.

But the biggest question that I had was, *Why?* What happened to make him leave me emotionally? I blamed myself: *You could have cooked him breakfast, lunch, and dinner like he expected you to do daily. Why didn't you clean up after him? You're his wife. Maybe you should have been more amenable to having sex every day, like he wanted.* I sulked. I went to work and came back home. I refused to go to church. I removed myself from our ministry. I began to eat whatever and whenever I wanted, and gained weight.

Usually happy-go-lucky at work, I couldn't bring myself to talk to anyone. I had nothing to say. I did my job and left. I began not to like myself and I loathed my husband.

Three weeks after I moved out, he served my dad the divorce papers. He expected me to bow out gracefully and let him move on with his life like we never existed. My dad! Really! That did it. Any hope I had of working things out and reconciling went out the window. I hired an attorney.

This is when I believe that God took over. Each time papers were filed in court, the other party had thirty days to respond. This process took approximately five months. It was during this time that things began to change. I went to Divorce Care, asked the Lord to help me heal and not be bitter, and asked the Lord to help me forgive so I could have a chance at life again, even if I had to remain single.

I remember driving home from work one day and saying out loud, "OK Lord, I'm open for whatever it is you have for me. If you want me to reconcile with my husband, which initially I was staunchly against, I am open to it. And if you want me to remain single, OK." It was at that moment that I felt totally free! Unforgiveness, hatefulness, and bitterness were extremely heavy. I still couldn't figure out the why of the demise of our marriage, so I decided that was OK. Too much of my life was being consumed by this situation. God was working.

A month later my phone rang. I'd finally unblocked my husband's phone number, so I recognized who the caller was. I was laughing when I answered the phone, and to this day I don't know why. He was sobbing uncontrollably. He loved me and apologized for all of the pain he'd put me through. The way he explained it, every night before bed, God let him feel the pain he'd inflicted on me. He also said that Satan had tried to destroy our marriage, using his mind, and that God had chastised him for allowing this. His next question was, Could I ever forgive him? I'd already forgiven him was my answer. We both understood that we had a long way to go, but he withdrew the divorce from court, paid my attorney off, and truly is a changed man. I can see this through his actions. After all, love is an action word.

8

A Warm, Pink Glow

Fran from Raleigh, North Carolina, USA
63 years old
Separated four months

Saturday morning, as I was deciding what to make for breakfast, my husband of thirty-eight years announced, "I'm leaving. I'm buying a townhouse." I knew by the sound of his voice and the look on his face that he meant it. For a man who for thirty-eight years wouldn't make a decision, this was a doozy. I was completely blindsided and devastated. A fog now swirling around my head and not a single cohesive thought could I find.

The next morning, he said, "I'm looking for an apartment. Do you want to go with me?" Was he kidding?? I said, "No." Five days later, on February 4, 2016, he moved out. The day before he planned to move out, I got a hotel room for myself and two of my best friends. The next day he texted me when he was done. One friend left for a family celebration. My other friend drove me home and stayed with me that night and the next day. She wouldn't let me walk back in the house, alone. Friends, dear wonderful friends. That's the only way I'm alive to tell this. To say I was in shock is putting it mildly. Nights were rough. I'd wake up around two or three in the morning, nauseous and shaking horribly. Then the sobbing would start. I'd either be up the rest of the night or fall back asleep from mental exhaustion.

The only thing helping to get me out of bed in the morning is my old kitty. Thank goodness she didn't lose her appetite like I had. I had to get up to feed her. For about two months, I could hardly eat anything. So at night, I'd fix a drink and it gave me a small appetite. I did talk to my doctor about it, and he said that was fine. I've lost a bit of weight and dropped a size or two. Yes it's a good thing but a heck of a way to do it. The only thing I could eat was comfort food. And, just like when I was pregnant, I went off coffee. (I was in shock then too.) And even scarier, I went off sweets! Along with all the strange eating issues, for at least the first two months, I felt like I had narcolepsy. I'd get through most my day and then all of a sudden I just couldn't hold my head up. I'd almost instantly fall asleep. Sometimes for ten minutes and other times for a few hours. The two hardest things for me at the start of this was the brain fog and the first holiday with us not being a family.

Early on, I made some changes in the house. I put my beautiful salt lamp on "his" nightstand. It casts a warm, pink glow with a dimmer switch. I placed a few beautiful quartz crystals on little stands around it. My bedroom is calm, serene, and welcoming.

At just three weeks into this nightmare, I went online to find something, anything that could help me survive this. I found the Runaway Husbands website and signed up for my local Healing Circle.

I soon received a group e-mail from Vikki asking us to please reach out to a new woman who had also just joined the Healing Circle. I didn't know what I could possibly do to help her when I was such a mess myself, but I reached out. Turns out, we're the same age, married the same year, one child, sons the same age and born in the same month. In her case, her husband did the more "normal" thing and left her for another woman. Mine left me for an empty apartment. She and I have become fast and very dear friends. I have an amazing support system of friends, but to also have a friend who is going through this at the same time is a godsend. We live near each other and talk and see each other often. We compare what our attorneys are saying. It's extremely helpful.

I volunteer at a non-profit retail store. I told them what happened to me and assured them if I couldn't be "professional" I wouldn't be there. I did my job slowly and carefully, but I don't remember much about those first two months. The people there are wonderful, supportive and there's always a hug when I need it. When I couldn't hold back the tears, I'd go to my car before they started. I'd cry and come back in.

Once I thought I was out there for maybe ten minutes. A friend came to check on me and told me I had been out there almost an hour!

Keeping busy was the most important thing for me, but I was honest with friends and asked them to please reach out to me. I just can't do the "reaching" right now. And they did. They still do. On the "home front," I had to start paying bills (another one of his jobs). A dear friend taught me to pay bills and do banking online. I did my car inspection and registration, more things I had never done. That was "his" department. And then, to make life even "better," just about a month or so after he left, I had a roof leak! Yes this was "his" area too. I called roofers, got estimates, etc., etc. I got it done.

He didn't just abandon me, he tore apart our little family. I keep contact with him to a minimum because it is so painful. It amazes me that somehow he has no concept of the hell he has thrown me into. No understanding of what his abandoning me has done. In my case he kept me in limbo for months, but finally, right before our thirty-ninth anniversary (and less than four months into this), he still thought it was his decision whether we stayed separated or not. But limbo was killing me and we talked. I told him I wouldn't take him back anyway after the way he treated me and disrespected me so let's move on.

I got my power back! And now I'm drinking coffee again! I drive at night. A week ago, I not only drove at night but in pouring rain! And I'm alive to tell the tale. Suicidal thoughts have stopped. I can't say I'm happy. But for the first time while out to breakfast with my son today, I felt, yes it was . . . happy. For a few minutes, life felt almost "normal." I didn't think either was ever going to be possible again. And yet here it is.

One more week and it will be four months since my "life partner" abandoned me. I have a new anniversary now—the fourth of each month. We are now about to enter into our negotiations. My head is much clearer. I don't cry nearly as much. I joined a support group and have a therapist. When he left, he couldn't answer my "Why?" But since then, he's told me he's "finding himself." At 63 I guess he's a late bloomer. One foot in front of the other. I'm beginning to believe there's light at the end of a very dark tunnel.

9

Weed, Guinness, and Watermelon

April from Portland, Oregon, USA
56 years old
Separated one year

We had been married almost twenty-six years and my husband had been working out of town, which he did quite often in construction. He had been gone two weeks and was back to spend a weekend together. He walked in, said "We need to talk." Then he told me that he had met a woman two weeks ago and they had been spending time together and he "wanted to see where it might go." I was just recovering from a bout of spring flu and thought that I was hallucinating. It did not seem real. It couldn't be. I asked if we could work it out. I asked if we could get counseling, and all he would say was, no, it's over, he wanted a divorce, it's been over a long time, he thought I felt that way too.

We have two grown daughters. The youngest had just moved out and they were living together two hours away. I got in the car and drove to be with them. I spent the weekend with my daughters and we comforted each other. We were all in shock and devastated. My husband was the guy everyone loved. I thought he was the nicest person in the world. I thought we were best friends.

I tried talking with my husband a few times over that weekend, on the phone and in e-mails, still trying to resolve or fix things. He said that he was done four or five years before and it had been over for a long time—that's why he had started working out of town more and more. I kept asking why he didn't tell me. He "didn't want to hurt me." What?

The thing that bothers me most is that when you read about this, the advice for avoiding it is to always "check in" with your marriage. Because my husband had been working out of town for about the last five to six years and at times there seemed to be a disconnect, I ALWAYS checked in. This was so unexpected! The month before, we had started the process of refinancing our home to use the equity to buy a rental property. We had been making plans for the future and empty nest years. This was SO unbelievable.

So he left, and I spent three months in the empty house, crying. It was summer and I couldn't eat or sleep, so I smoked a lot of weed (legal in Oregon) to get to sleep at night and drank Guinness and ate watermelon. I lost thirty pounds. I read everything I could find on the Internet and found Vikki's book. It helped a lot to know that this wasn't unusual and that I wasn't stupid. I woke up every morning, my heart racing and in a complete state of panic with the thought that this was really happening. This lasted over a year, and it still happens. I am currently wearing a heart monitor to see if there is something wrong, but it's likely PTSD, panic attacks.

My biggest concern was that I was 55 and had not worked in four years. I have a B.S. in education but need the grad program for a certified teaching job. I had worked many years as an educational assistant, so I immediately started applying for jobs for the fall school year. We lived on five acres in the woods, outside a small town in central/western Oregon. I loved it there. I had designed the house and we had built it together, but I knew that I couldn't afford to keep it and being there just made me feel sad and lonely. So I prepared for the move and applied for jobs in Portland, closer to my daughters.

I went to many interviews and filled out several applications and did not get hired right away, as I had when I was younger. Honestly, I had never had a job interview that I didn't get hired from. There were several rejections and this really scared me. The school year started and I still didn't have a job, I did get on the pool for substitute teachers, and in Portland that gives you work every day but it doesn't give you benefits. Luckily, two weeks into the term, a para-educator quit. I got an interview and got the job!!!

I squeezed in with my daughters for a couple months, until I found my own place. He had left me in May, and the divorce was final in February. I got about seventy-five percent of everything and a decent amount of spousal support. Guilt worked in my favor. We got the house on the market in April and it sold for full price in two days. I had been living back and forth and was not quite ready for that, but now it feels better, sort of like ripping the bandage off.

It has now been just over a year. Having my own place helps. Working full time helps. Therapy helps. Acupuncture, massage, mani/pedis, walking the dogs, helps. Girlfriends help, especially the divorced ones. Making plans for the future helps. I will be going to graduate school in a few weeks to get my teaching licensure. College at 56 seems crazy at times but it will double my income, and the uncertainty of spousal support continuing makes me nervous so I will be better off this way.

Changing my name back and getting that done on everything was tedious and took a lot longer than I wanted, but it also helps. Self-care is important. Remove him and reminders from your life as much as possible. I had family pictures on the wall and printed out pictures of George Clooney and Johnny Depp and taped their faces over his. (This also provided some good laughs.) I removed him from all social media. Cry as much as you want. Try to keep your sense of humor and don't get lost in the sadness.

I still have moments when I just don't believe this is happening I think, *This isn't my life; I can't believe he did this!* I am constantly reminded by friends and therapists that there was nothing I could have done differently and that this was a huge betrayal so I could not have seen it coming. It's easy to look back and see things that might have been signs, but when you say to the person, "Are we OK? Do we need to talk about this?" and he says everything is fine, you want to believe the person you have loved and trusted for twenty-six years.

10

Who Are You?

Elizabeth from Florida, USA
68 years old
Separated five months

Forty-six years of loving and being loved by my husband—then suddenly abandoned . . .

The love of my life had been a physician, one of the best, specializing in the care of women. Six years prior he had been diagnosed with a very manageable autoimmune disease but one that did not allow him the dexterity to continue with his surgery. Ultimately he retired. When friends asked him what he would do in retirement, he told them that he would swim and lift weights. He would tell me that he additionally was going to retire to me!

My profession is design. I was enjoying what I was doing, had become very good at it, and consequently had the jobs and clients that one waits a lifetime to achieve. I had spent years raising two wonderful and successful sons. I did not want to retire just yet.

We had two homes. I finally was working on what I was referring to as my last and best career job. The work required me me to travel back and forth between two locations, but I was away from him as little as possible.

With my support he found a group that he could work out with in the city where we reside in the winter months. I was highly encouraging and enjoyed very much the people he was swimming with on a social scale, as swimming had been an activity that had initially brought us together years earlier. I encouraged him to continue, bought him a new cell phone, and taught him to text. He seemed happy and content while I was working—supporting me while I pursued my final job, doing what I loved.

Over a three-month period this past year, it became apparent to me that one of the divorced females (ten years younger) in the swimming group had developed some kind of an "emotional" attachment to my husband. I never worried, as he was a good and faithful partner and always had my utmost trust. However, this odd infiltration of this woman had become so evident to me that we had three different discussions about the fact that I believed her to be somewhat invading our lives. He was defensive, accusing me of not trusting him . . . but, why would I not?

As several months progressed into January, he became distant from me. He was not his same loveable self—no longer carrying my bags, no longer paying so much attention to me, no longer showering me with the warmth and affection that had become the hallmark of our many years together, no gifts at Christmas. I merely thought him to be suffering from depression, a depression that had perhaps been with him since his retirement but one he refused to admit to, refusing professional help.

When I walked into our bedroom one morning, he suddenly jumped with the cell phone in his hand and then immediately hid it under his legs. Stunned, I walked out of the room, only to turn around and walk back in, asking what he was doing, with whom was he texting? At that instant on January 22, 2016, at 11:40 a.m. he bolted upright, literally screamed that he wanted a divorce, grabbed a bag, several items, stormed out of the house, and left me.

My heart was beating out of my chest. What the hell had just happened?

I called my sister. She immediately came over and, perhaps, was in as much disbelief as I. I called my good friend. I ultimately changed the locks. My sister kept me with her the rest of the day. My husband called me early that afternoon. I did not answer. At three in the afternoon, he called once again. I picked up the phone to listen to him ask me how I was doing. I inquired of him, "How do you think I would be doing? Where are you staying?" His response was that I did not need to know. I hung up. I knew very well where he was. I thought I would not live another day.

Upon her insistence, I stayed with my sister that night. She happened to be renting a residence immediately across the street from where my husband and I were living.

At two in the morning, I received several phone calls and messages from my husband. He had driven over, was furious that I had changed the locks and wanted me to know that, since our property was still jointly owned, I had no right to do so, and in fact if I did not either meet and let him in or give him a key, he would have the sheriff over in the morning to open the door for him. I called him back and did meet him there. It was approximately 3:30 a.m. When he stormed in, he thanked me for allowing him in, grabbed clothes, raced through the living room where I was sitting and said, "You are going to hate me. You are going to hate me." When I asked exactly why then he was doing this to us, his response was, "Because I am a schmuck! I am a schmuck!"

Minutes later he sat down to tell me that we needed to stay civil with each other, as we would be resolving this divorce via mediation and that he had no intentions of denying me of anything less than half of all we had earned together. My mouth had dropped open—I was in shock. How long had he had planned this escape?

In summary, I am 68 years old, as is he. It has been exactly four months since my once faithful and loving partner became one more "Runaway Husband," and I the "Abandoned Wife." We are scheduled for our second mediation session this week.

We have e-mailed frequently—at first for me to totally vent my rage, and he to attempt to explain to me why exactly his pathetic behavior was all my fault: I was too busy working. I did not notice his mounting depression. I was not there for him. I was not swimming with him. I was not riding in the golf cart with him.

He needed to find an excuse to validate his bad behavior, when in actuality it was ultimately his missing his adoring patients and his admiring colleagues and his shrinking lack of self-esteem—all the while I was perhaps the happiest I'd been, and merely months away from retirement.

He just could not wait. He said it was "too late"!

When paying our joint cell phone bill for the first time after his sudden departure, I looked at his text usage and shockingly noted that he had 4,780 text messages between him and his affair partner in the last thirty-day billing cycle. Checking further, it appeared this relationship began steamrolling months before.

To say these past four months have been difficult would be an understatement. However, I am blessed with a multitude of good friends and family. That has been my key, and that has been my salvation. I do know this will be a long process for me, and it will take time—probably years. It seems to me it is rather like dealing with a death. Yet, it would have been easier if he had died. I would have been left with the memories of the good person that he had been.

I think I am being so strong and doing so well, but then I will just cry, out of the blue, just cry. I will have to live the rest of my life with his betrayal. On the other hand, he will have to live the rest of his life knowing the person he has become. I do not know which will be more difficult.

11

Digging New Neural Trenches

Virginia from Anchorage, Alaska, USA
51 years old
Separated two years

I see it now, in hindsight. The haircuts every three weeks. The $300 jeans. Riding a skateboard around downtown, even though he was 40 years old. But I didn't see it then. He'd seemed a bit distant, but then he'd been working long hours six days a week for over five years, trying to get his restaurant off the ground. I just thought he was tired, and I was doing him a favor by not nagging him. We still tell each other "I love you" every day.

Then he sat down and said, all in one sentence, "I don't think I love you the way a man should love the woman he's married to, and I don't think I ever have [sixteen years], and so I don't think we're worth trying to save."

Not surprisingly, it took a minute for those words to sink in, but when they did, I felt like my very body was coming apart. I shook, I cried, I wanted to throw up. He seemed genuinely surprised. "I thought you felt the same way," he said.

"Is there someone else?" I asked. He said, "No"—but of course there was. A cute little waitress from his restaurant who was also divorcing her husband. She was 25 years old. I was just about to turn 50.

I realized it when I dragged him, kicking and screaming, into the marriage counselor's office. This must just be a misunderstanding, I thought. Something he's going through that I can't understand or fix, but I'll find someone who can fix us. Overall, I thought the session (he only attended one session) went well. He said some nice things about me, about us. I thought we could iron it out and move on, maybe even be stronger than we were before. Then at the end, the counselor proposed an exercise we could work on for a month and then have another session. The look in my husband's eyes—a month? No, he couldn't do that, he said. The counselor backpedaled, OK, then, two weeks. Same look. After sixteen years, he wouldn't even spend two weeks working on our marriage. I knew then that there was another woman, and he couldn't wait to be with her.

How nonchalant and happy he seemed. I, on the other hand, couldn't eat, couldn't sleep, and lost fifteen pounds. If you're reading this, you already know. It happens to all of us, evidently.

I found and devoured *Runaway Husbands*. I read it a second time, then a third. It all seemed so surreal that just knowing it happened to other people was such a relief. Everyone in my social circle knew us as a happy couple; surely I must have known. But I didn't. I was blindsided. Earthquake. Tidal wave. Whatever analogy of abrupt and total devastation, it was that.

I read a bunch of other self-help books, too. Books on narcissism, and rejection, and betrayal. He'd been my best friend. Of all the things he could have done, I would never have expected this from him.

Ultimately, as painful as it is to think of having wasted sixteen years of my life chasing down someone who didn't love me back, not in "that way," I do think he was telling the truth. Ours was a relationship of mutual respect and friendship, love and support. But it was never "fiery" or "passionate." I thought that's what mature love could be, but he wanted something else, maybe precisely as he was turning 40.

Maybe he is a narcissist, too, chasing after the next "shiny object." And maybe in his new relationship, he gets to be dominant to his much younger girlfriend. I don't know if she knows (or cares) that the reason he's a successful business owner is because I bought that business for him. But in our own marriage, we were equals, and maybe he wanted to be the boss. Honestly, I've mostly come to realize I don't know anything about him, including exactly why he left. I doubt if he knows it himself. He was never especially big on introspection.

But it was clear there was no turning back. He wasn't going to come begging me to change my mind, so according to all the self-help books, I had to reinvent a life for myself without him. And that is something I'm still working on. I have tried all of the following things in the past two years: yoga, exercise, running, therapy, talking to friends, burying myself in work, reading self-help books, journaling, Xanax, meditation, website chat rooms. I have stayed in the same town because I didn't want to feel like he drove me out of this town, but I have decided after two years that I need a new start and I can't do that here.

Of the things listed above, they all worked, a little. The thing that worked the best was to just keep moving, "dig new neural trenches," as my friend said. After so many years, a lot of "us" was just habit, and I had to make new habits, substitute things we did together with things I did on my own. I forced myself to attend Meetup groups, where no one knew me as half of us—so painful and awkward at first, easier now.

Most shocking was that I lost most of the friends we had as a couple. I couldn't bear the idea that somehow my single life was being com- pared to his newly ecstatic coupled one, that I was being compared to his new girlfriend, whether my friends were actually doing so or not. And most of them took his side—or refused to take sides, which to me was the same thing. He was, after all, easier to be around, happy in love with the new girl.

Words of hope? It gets better, but it takes time. You may never really understand why it happened, and at some point you have to stop trying. That story lies behind you now and you need to focus on your own story. Stop thinking about him. Stop thinking about THEM. You don't know anything about him or them. These are the stories we tell ourselves, with no evidence to support them. It's very, very hard at first—at least it was for me—but it does get better, easier, to find your path. At two years, I'm still trying. I'm still sad. And that's OK; it just means the marriage meant something to me and so I grieve its loss. But I no longer think it had anything to do with me. And so I'm off to set up my own new life, whatever that may hold.

12

He Went to the Toilet and Never Came Back!

Janet from Leicester, England, UK
51 years old
Separated six years

It was a beautiful, sunny June afternoon. My husband had just come back from his usual Sunday motorcycle ride and went straight into the bath. I sat on the bathroom floor talking to him about his day, then went into the garden and lit the barbecue. My children—Abigail, then 19, and Thomas, 15—were enjoying the afternoon all together in the garden. My husband asked me where his phone charger was. I didn't know. He became very irrational and anxious. I told him not to worry, it would be somewhere around. A few minutes later, we were all sitting in deckchairs in the garden and he told me he was going to the toilet. I sat and sat and eventually I went inside, Thomas was watching TV. I asked him if he had seen his dad, and he said no. I looked outside, and his car had gone. I was totally confused: Where had he gone? I texted him and rang him. No answer.

Approximately two hours later, after hearing nothing, I left a voice message on his phone, telling him that if he didn't answer my calls I would ring the police, as I was getting worried about him. He immediately rang me. I remember it like it was yesterday—I was in the bathroom. I remember him saying he wasn't coming back, that he was leaving me for someone who he had met at work. I remember what I can only describe as a howl, and collapsing on the bathroom floor. He put the phone down and immediately rang my sister to come over to me because he had just told me he was leaving me and I was in a state. He'd left in the shorts and T-shirt he was wearing.

The days that followed were a haze. My brother and his wife came over and stayed with me. The doctor put me on tablets and I had a week off work. I remember that for the first week all I did was cry, drink tea, and go to the toilet—I didn't eat or sleep. He came over the next week and all I remember doing is screaming in his face. I remember my spit actually hitting his face and he didn't even flinch. He was my entire world—I'd lost my mum in 2004 and my dad in 2007. I didn't think there was a pain greater than that, but this topped it all.

Here I am six years later and I am full of total hatred for this man. I have had to reinvent myself, get two jobs to support myself. My daughter had counselling at university, which helped—she considers herself to no longer have a father. My son is now a 21-year-old man. He has grown up to be a very angry person. He wouldn't have any help. He has started seeing "him" in the last two years, but it's not the same. They meet on a Wednesday for a few hours. It is just so, so sad.

I have had counselling but I don't think it has helped. I cannot and will not forgive him, and I feel that if I start to forget then that means I have forgiven him—and I have far too much hatred to ever forgive him. In 2013, he bought himself a brand new Ducati and on 15 August 2013, as he was going to work, he was involved in an accident with a lorry. He went under it and came out the other side with one arm! And do you know what? That still isn't enough for me! That is the depth of hurt he was caused me.

I am proud of what I achieve every single day. I run a car, a home, have two beautiful children, a gorgeous grandson, but I so miss and yearn for the family unit that we no longer have. He has denied me and my children of so many things. Life is so hard for me now—I have very little confidence and I find it very hard to trust anyone. He has totally left us in complete devastation and there he is living his life. I will never recover from what he did—I hope one day he feels the pain we have.

Can I think of any funny moments? I remember clearing all his after-shave out, and while I was doing it, the doorbell rang. It was the postman with a parcel. I gave him his aftershave, after telling him my story. You have to laugh. People don't believe me when I tell them he went to the toilet and never came back. Maybe that's why I can't move on. I've never had closure, or answers. I didn't even know there was anything wrong with my marriage. We were holding hands shopping the day before. We had sex on the Saturday night. The hurt is with me every single day. I am so dreadfully hurt, and here I am six years later and I still cry for the life we had. I still cry for my children and the things they have missed out on.

I still cry for the complete, utter waste of what he did. But I do feel that I am a nicer person now; I don't know how. When I look back now, I didn't like the person I was when I was with him. I appreciate life more too. I don't know why he did what he did. He was a great dad. I didn't think he was capable of putting his own happiness ahead of his children's. He never gave us a chance to put things right—he just went. I will never forgive him for that.

13

Suddenly Single and 40 . . .
Need I Say More?

Kerry from Fairhaven, Massachusetts, USA
41 years old
Separated eighteen months

On September 1, 2014, my husband and I were sitting on our front porch and out of the blue he told me he wanted a separation. I told him he must be joking, as we never even fought before. He said that he felt that we hadn't been getting along that well and he needed more space. I said, "Space for what? To date?" He said no, he just wanted to be alone. I asked if he was moving out or if he was asking me to move out. He said he didn't know. Nothing made sense in that moment, but I said let's continue to talk and work on this every night. I told him I loved him.

I didn't really take the conversation very seriously at all because he came to bed that night and all was fine. We continued to talk over the next two nights. Three days later I got a phone call from a mutual friend of ours saying that they were sorry to hear about our separation. I asked who told them about it. They said they heard it from my husband! I later found out from this friend that he had a mistress, they were engaging in unprotected sex, and he even bragged about how he kept slippers at her house!

I called my husband at work to come home and we got into an argument. He told me they were just having an emotional affair because he needed someone to talk to and that I wasn't around enough. I kicked the ottoman over and he called the police on me! I was mortified. In my 39 years, I'd never had any trouble with the law. He told the police I was inside tearing up the house. The officer came in and asked if either of us had a place to stay that night. My husband willingly offered to leave and said he'd be back that weekend.

That day he left and I never heard from him again. He moved in with his girlfriend that night and served me with divorce papers the following week. Our family and friends were shocked to say the very least. This was such unusual behavior for a man who loved the town he lived in, loved his job, loved his house and I thought loved me. He had even recently moved in his own mother right next door to us. I'll never to this day understand why he left in such a cowardly way, although he was always a mama's boy.

Luckily I have great parents, family, and friends that I could lean on and that were there for me from the very beginning. I also went to see a therapist right away and continued doing that over the next six months. I made an appointment with my doctor and he put me on an antidepressant and sleeping pill. I didn't want to take medication, but I needed a short-term solution. My co-workers even rallied around me and found me the best lawyer possible.

The way I moved on was by just relying on everyone around me and throwing myself into the divorce process, which proved to be very long. I would say I felt more shock than sadness over those next three months. I would wake up each morning, sitting straight up and out of breath because the bed would be empty. Then I'd feel for my diamond on my ring finger that wasn't there anymore.

Through this process I learned to be very independent. The cleaning service was the first to go because of the divorce, but I did find a sense of calm cleaning this big gigantic house I was left in by myself. I went food shopping by myself. I serviced my car by myself. I took the cat to the vet by myself. I fixed things around the house by myself. (Google became my best friend.) I even learned to go out to dinner by myself.

I live in a very small town, and my sudden pending divorce was the topic of everyone's gossip and conversation. One night a woman recognized my face and said, "OMG, I know you! Aren't you that girl that was married to that guy that left you for that biker looking chick?" I had become that girl whose husband left for a bar whore.

Some other things that helped were staying in a routine. I continued working out and I even took up kickboxing, which was very exciting and a great stress reliever. I also spend lots of time with my family, and now we have dinner and a sleepover every Monday night, which I look forward to.

After a few months I became restless and bored and wanted some excitement in my life. I was angry that my ex was running all around town with this woman while I was sitting home, so I joined a dating website. I didn't even know if men would find me attractive, but it turned out to be a fun and exciting experience. There are a lot of lunatics out there and lots of men only interested in sex, but I did meet one man who I'm still dating to this day, eighteen months later.

I did ponder for many months, *Why did he leave me?* I had no clue. No warning. No obvious signs this was going to happen. I explained my story to a male co-worker and he simply said; "Your husband just fell out of love with you." It's as simple as that. Once you learn to accept that, you can move on. He was right. It was true. He didn't love me anymore.

There were lots of good and bad moments. One of my lows was posting my ex's girlfriend's picture and my story to a website called shesa-homewrecker.com, which I wouldn't recommend doing! Apparently she applied for a job, and they did a background check on her—and my post came up. Oops! Needless to say, she didn't get the job.

I would say I'm more of a pessimist now, but I think that's OK. I can say that in general I don't trust men, but maybe someday my feelings will change. I hope so. My new attitude is, "There's the door if you don't like it" and the only person I have to please is myself, but here's what I learned over the last eighteen months:

1. You can be around a person for a long time, but that doesn't mean you know them.

2. If something doesn't seem right, it probably isn't. Woman's intuition is very powerful.
3. Communication is the most important part of any relationship. You have to communicate your feelings and check in with each other every single day.
4. Having your partner as your best friend is not enough—there has to be passion too.
5. Your mom can see your fake friends before you do. I will never make unworthy people a priority in my life again. Family comes first, always.
6. You can live with less than you think. Material things don't make you truly happy.
7. Everything happens for a reason and time heals all wounds. Have faith and keep moving forward.

14

Putting One Foot in Front of the Other

Susan from San Francisco, California, USA
52 years old
Separated 6 years

In the summer of 2009 my then husband told me he didn't love me anymore. This was a complete shock. We had just hosted his family from abroad, and upon leaving they remarked on how happy we were. And I was. No marriage is perfect, but I thought our marriage was solid. We talked with each other, managed our respective jobs, spent time with family and friends. We were able to have "tough" conversations about the stepchildren and where we wanted to be in our lives going forward.

How did my husband tell me this? We were in bed, about to go to sleep, when I murmured as I usually do, "I love you. Nite." Silence from my husband. I thought maybe he had fallen asleep or maybe he hadn't heard me, so I said it again. He had heard me and said, "I don't love you anymore."

I was devastated. The next few months were a blur. We went to a marriage counselor, where we talked about the ups and downs of marriage, the ebbs and flow of life. He was adamant that he was never going to love me again. He finally left for good after a session with our marriage counselor—I didn't even know that he had packed up that day to leave, as we had driven separate cars to the counselor's office. I still remember the hiccupping cries as I sat in my car after that session and my husband had driven away. The hiccupping cries continued for several years.

Forward to today.

What helped?

Well of course Vikki did—and I did attend one of Vikki's workshops in Montreal a few years ago. Meeting and speaking with other women who were in the same position helped tremendously.

Second—just putting one foot in front of the other. My life was a blur for the first couple of years—and the intense physical pain in the pit of my stomach lasted for almost five years.

Third—talking about it with a therapist helped me to believe that it wasn't my fault that I had missed the "signs"—there were no signs to miss. And of course talking it through with my best friends helped as well.

Finally—just the passage of time. Yes, it still hurts—but not nearly as much as it used to. It no longer knocks me for a loop when I see a social media posting from my stepdaughter that includes my ex and his new "15-years-younger-than-me" wife. I just laugh it off.

My heart goes out to every woman who goes through this—and I say to each one of you beautiful, talented women: "You are strong. You will survive. Life will get better. It may take time—and for some (like me) more time, but I promise—it will get better.

15

My Dog, Louie, Got it Right!

Sophie from New York State, USA
53 years old
Separated four years

My name is Sophie. I reside in upstate New York with my four children and an old English bulldog named Louie. I'm 51 years old, starting over after my husband of twenty-four years left me for another women. I don't know what hurt the most, the fact that the man I was still in love with was having a three-year affair or the simple fact that he had no trouble walking out on our life together.

At first I missed him insanely and tried to win him back, spending most of my time "re-inventing" myself trying to create a "perfect" wife. All my efforts were pointless. He moved on, never missing a beat. It had been over three years and I had to face the fact. For the first time in my life, I was scared. I was always a strong woman with a sassy overlay, but this was something I could not move past easily. But why? I'd experienced anguish before and made it through the haze but, for the first time, I walked around feeling defeated and speechless. My ex would visit the children, looking so happy and unaffected, while I was so de-natured by the split.

Friends and family tried their best to keep my mind off of the sad moments. But I just could not escape the memories and the feelings of failure. I expected to grow old with this man, but did I really know my husband? How did he become this person? Then one day, my youngest son came home from school and said, "Mom, we learned about chameleons today. They change to meet the needs of the moment. My teacher said it's all about adapting, right?"

Then it hit me. I needed to stop punishing myself and shed the sadness. Every night, I would lie in bed and imagine a visionary change. As the layers slide down to the floor, it exposed new, stronger skin that was ready to live, love, and once again be that intelligent, sassy woman. After much reflection and journal writing, I realized this writer needed an editor.

I started dating and joining groups that smudged my comfort line. To my surprise, I quickly became aligned with the changes. Never looking back. I am still single but no longer lonely. Two of my children are established and launched; the younger two are with me fifty percent. It is a very amicable arrangement. Oh, and my ex . . . yeah, you guessed it. His gal cheated on him and left with a younger man. He was devastated and tried to come home, but I had the locks changed and Louie bit him when he tried to get in. I suppose my ex thought it was a sign and never asked to come home again. (I always liked that dog . . . lol.)

Funny, I thought I would get great pleasure out of his demise, but I didn't. It's just not my style. However, I never considered taking him back. How does the saying go? "Once awaking from the dream, you can't go back to sleep." I liked my wake-up call and my new skin—it looks great on me!

💔

16

Life Is about Choice and Gratitude

Karen from Iowa, USA
59 years old
Separated four years

Chuck and I married in August 1981. Our divorce was finalized in December 2012.

Thirty-one years, which I and literally everyone else thought, were years exemplary of a great marriage. However, one Saturday in March of 2012, I learned that I could not have been more wrong about our relationship and the character of my husband. Seven days later he had moved out of our beautiful family home and in with one of his employees. She was a woman whom he had known only seven months.

Chuck and I met in March of 1980. He had just moved and came to my office for telephone service. It was a very busy day. I noticed that he waited for me to finish with my customers to ensure I helped him next. He asked me out for a date. I uncharacteristically accepted a date from a customer. We went out that evening and grew to be good friends. From there, our romantic relationship began.

In March of 1981, Chuck proposed to me. We were married in August that year. We soon settled in to a marriage that, by anyone's account, was a great one. I continued to work and enjoyed success as a business office manager and corporate trainer. We both enjoyed travel, and my work afforded us many frequent flyer points. Vacations took us all over the country. At the same time, Chuck continued to build his business. The company grew from very humble beginnings thanks to Chuck's hard work.

We were blessed with three sons. Our oldest was born in 1988. As we had also planned, I took a break from my career to stay home with our son. Our second son arrived in 1990 and son number three in 1993.

Things could not have been better. My husband's business continued to grow. We purchased a large acreage with woods and a delightful creek. In 1995, we built a beautiful new home. What a great place to raise three boys! We were abundantly blessed. As a Christian family, we attended church regularly. It seemed as though there were no "chinks in the armor" of our marriage. Our relationship had a strong foundation based on our faith, our early and continuing friendship, and our commitment to each other. Our children were healthy and happy. Chuck continued to work very hard for our family.

In May 1997, I returned to work. A local utility company offered a part-time job with full benefits. That decision would become one of the best things I ever, ever did for myself.

Life continued on. Our three sons graduated high school and went off to college. Son number one was in his final semester of college and son number two in his second year when the figurative bomb went off.

Truly, neither I nor any of my friends can think of a time when there were any indications that my marriage was about to come undone. None whatsoever. One hears of women giving birth, claiming they never they knew they were pregnant. Hard to believe! Nevertheless, that is how shocked I felt when I learned my marriage was ending. I was totally blindsided, bewildered, and deeply, deeply hurt. It was hard for me to believe!

One Saturday afternoon in March of 2012, I dropped by my husband's office. He had been at work for a while that day and I stopped in to say hello. I parked in back and walked to the office in front of the building. The lights were off. This was not unusual, as he had a large, adjacent warehouse in which he often worked. When I opened the front door to his dark office, I found him embracing Sheila! Sheila, the woman he had hired the previous August to work as a salesperson. A salesperson indeed! The woman is literally a former drug user, convicted felon, and three-time divorcee. She is also three years my senior. Chuck knew of her criminal record. When he realized they had been found out, Chuck's words were, "Moment of truth!"

Instantly my knees went weak. Chuck was not the type of person to hug any woman other than me or his own mother. I knew I had witnessed infidelity. I could hardly speak. My mouth was dry. I asked, "What is going on? After thirty years . . . What are you doing?" Sheila quickly exited. Chuck sat down to speak to me. I could see that the "switch had flipped." He was no longer the same person. I could tell. His demeanor and the way he spoke to me were foreign. I again asked what was going on and why he was now speaking to me in that manner. He said he no longer had to "put up a front."

I did not sleep that night. Not one wink. Monday morning rolled around and I debated whether to remain in bed in the fetal position or get up and face the day. I got up and went to work. My employer's employee assistance plan referred me to a counselor with whom I met four times. The sessions helped me to see things that I could not otherwise see due to the fog and devastation I was experiencing.

Our relationship had come to an end. One week later, on April 7, 2012, Chuck moved out of our home and in with Sheila. I filed for divorce in May, and the divorce was finalized in December of 2012.

The prayers and support of my friends were critical to my survival. It was a very difficult time. I cried regularly. I sold my beautiful home and moved to town in the span of five months. In the aftermath of the divorce, I went back to college. For my own self-edification, I completed two master's degrees, in business administration and organizational leadership. My studies helped to pass the time and gave me a sense of accomplishment and increased self-esteem.

My employer was discreet and supportive. My career has taken off. In the four years since the divorce, I have been promoted four times and more than doubled my salary. I continue to be abundantly blessed.

To this day, I do not know why things ended. Chuck has never told me his reasons for the breakup. The fact that my life plans were so violently changed is still hard to deal with. The loneliness from the loss and betrayal by the man I thought was my very best friend and most trusted confidant remains difficult to accept. Yet, the pain continues to diminish as time passes.

I realize life is always about choices and gratitude. I continue to choose happiness and am thankful for the blessings in my life. Keeping things in perspective and focusing on the good has been critical for me.

17

I'm a Good Person and So Are You

Kay from East Rochester, New York, USA
59 years old
Separated five years

It was Friday, September 3, 2010, 9:00 a.m. I had been planning for our 29th anniversary (September 12th)—he had not! That fateful morning I awoke and went downstairs to discover he had not gone to work. I asked if he was staying home for the day. No, he was not. But he wanted to talk to me in the living room. We sat down across from each other, and without looking at me, he pulled a sheet of paper from his pocket and read to me that he was going his own way, that "we" should take care in how "we" told the children, and that we would remain close friends, with each enjoying our own separate lives.

Stunned, I went upstairs, got dressed, and left the house. I drove to the college where my younger daughter was enrolled and told her he was leaving me. She responded with unbearable sorrow. I called my older daughter and asked if she could meet us at the college. She agreed, and when she arrived I told her the same news. She responded with uncontainable fury. They took care of me that day as I gasped for breath and grasped for any kind of reality.

In the days that followed I felt like I was free-floating in air, with no solid ground under my feet and no compass pointing in any direction. I had lost EVERYTHING! I was unemployed. Not a single "friend" stepped forward to help or console, but rather they all disappeared into the murk. I had no home. I felt my whole life had been snatched from me. The family I had worked so hard for had been shattered, never to be the close-knit family I had thought it was. Everything was a sham. It felt he had stolen thirty-two years of my life that I could never get back.

And he wasn't finished. I moved into a small apartment to get away from him, as he came back five days after he left, saying he had nowhere to go, and we'd live together as friends until the divorce was finalized. I was amazed how very quickly my deep love and commitment to him turned to hatred and loathing. As deeply as I had loved, was now as deeply as I hated him, and that took me by horrible surprise to know those kinds of feelings resided within me.

He dragged the process out for over four years, in uncooperative behavior, until finally his lawyer had to communicate to me through my lawyer in order to get the information he needed to end this hellish situation. His lawyer said to him, "You started this. Now you have to end it, and give her her life back. What you are doing is cruel!!!" I don't know how the lawyers finally got him to sign the final papers, but when I finally got word that it was over, I felt like I had been released from a cage!

To this day I do not know why he did what he did. He told me that his leaving me was all my fault, but he refused to tell me what I had done to deserve the destruction of my world that he brought on by his unilateral decision.

I moved on by purchasing an old home and renovating it—making it mine, my haven, my safe place. I met a woman in a store, who saw me breakdown as I was trying to purchase a miter saw to do some woodworking. She was a manager and she took me to a back room and told me about *Runaway Husbands*. She told me I wasn't alone. That it had happened to her too. I was so very grateful to her and I was astounded that such a thing had happened to anyone else. I immediately got the book and read it from cover to cover in one sitting. I think my mouth was agape in astonishment the entire time. It was as if this unknown woman had been standing beside me throughout my entire ordeal, taking notes. This was ME she was writing about!!!

I found the website and subscribed to the newsletter. Just knowing there were others out there who had gone through the same devastation helped me. My heart hurt for every woman out there! No one should be subjected to such cruelty!

Now I have a wonderfully kind psychiatrist who is treating me for the PTSD that occurred due to the Wife Abandonment Syndrome I was experiencing. Even having a name to call this horrible situation helped me. I am also seeing a lovely DBT therapist who is teaching me how to detect and to avoid abusive people. It has been, and continues to be, very hard work. I have learned to listen and observe even more closely than I could before. I have learned to find my innermost self and to abide by what I need. I have finally even dared to date again, but I do so without expectation. One date at a time, enjoying the moment—learning, deciding, as each moment passes, Is this right for me or no? And finding the courage to walk away or continue on, depending on what my innermost self tells me.

I have become much more self-aware but also much more aware of people and their actions and what those actions mean. I try hard to take everything I observe and turn it into a learning experience—a way to grow and gain wisdom, but also a way to protect myself and to try to find a safer path and a safer life for myself. I hope that when I am truly recovered, I will have surrounded myself with a small group of people who truly care about me. No more sham relationships or abusive people within my circle!

Being abandoned is a very hurtful event that shakes you down to your very core. It makes you question all things, and makes you wonder what is really true and what is not—what is real and what is a lie. It is sometimes very hard to go on. Many, many times I have not wanted to, but here I am, still pushing forward. Here is what I know though. I am a good person, and so are you. I did nothing wrong, and neither did you. I am determined to grow and become an even better person than I was before. And I am eventually going to find the person who will cherish me for a lifetime, whether as a companion or a spouse.

The new people I have met have commented on my kindness and quiet humor, on my determination and my honesty. They have recognized my patience and my good nature, my gentle spirit and my creativity. It had been there all the time—all those years. It was not me. Yes, I'm sure I made mistakes, but how can you address them if you are not told about them? The people who know me now also know that I would have addressed and tried to correct any misunderstanding or hurt before they became untenable. It wasn't me . . . or you.

18

I Don't Want a New Normal;
I Want My Old Normal!

Jo from Ashland, Oregon, USA
46 years old
Separated three years

I would love to tell this story. I think it would be cathartic. I probably shouldn't try to do this right now, as I don't have much time, but . . . I was in a twenty-two-year relationship. Some of you may discount it, because it was a gay relationship, but you shouldn't, because all the feeling and experiences of loss and grief are absolutely no different.

It seems I notice a lot of divorces near the twenty-year mark. Not sure what that's about, but . . . my ex, we'll call her Bob . . . on October 26, 2012, seeming out of nowhere, she said, "I'm done." I didn't know what that meant. Was she done with the dishes, done washing her car? I had no idea what she was talking about. I do not remember the exact words after that—I just remember somehow she made it clear she was referring to the relationship.

About eight years prior, we had adopted two beautiful children. They had some issues. Her work had some upheavals I tried to be supportive through. But about three year prior to her leaving, in hindsight, I noticed some changes in behavior. I truly don't think she was cheating, at least with a person, but the changes in how she chose to use her time felt like infidelity.

For three years I tried to pick up the ball, doing what we often did together with the kids' appointments on my own, thinking she needed to focus more on her work or that something seemed to be stressing her out. The year prior I had thrown her a party for her 50th birthday. I thought that I just needed to work on carrying more weight. Her behavior was odd, but I shrugged it off, just trying to keep the family going.

At first she tried to get me to move out, telling me she would give me money, etc. Well she is not good with money management and tried to get me to work it all out through a guy at our church who was probably more of a friend to her than to me. I decided I was not going to let the kids think that I was the one that left, because they were young and it would have been easy to perceive that I was the one who abandoned them. I was not. I was not going to let her midlife crisis do that and kick me out of my home.

I was devastated—almost mortally wounded. The pain was indescribable, which I feel a little guilty about, because I know so many are going through so much worse. And yet, the person (myself) whom I usually view as compassionate and concerned about my local area and the world at large had nothing left to give, no compassion, no sympathy— just grief and pain.

I was so completely self-absorbed in my life and my grief that no one else existed. Again, not something I am proud of, but it was all I could do to put one foot in front of the other. Because of her threats to take the kids, I finally signed the divorce papers and agreed with the parenting plan although I was not sure if that was the right thing to do. I have learned that when she makes threats like that, the best thing to do is to tell her, "Bob, do what you need to do." It got to a point where I was tired of being threatened and bullied, because she is a bully.

The two years following were the toughest two years of my life. I hit some pretty rough spots in those two years, and I was not sure I was going to make it. People talked about the new normal and I wanted to punch them. I wanted my old normal. I wanted my family made whole. My son, almost four years later, still tries to get us together. It's like that Disney movie *The Parent Trap*. I ache for my kids.

All I could do in those two years was care for my kids (whom she made it difficult to have time with because of my work schedule) and get myself to work and home. In that same two year period, both of my dogs and two of my cats died. The divorce was devastating. I lost thirty-four pounds and got down to ninety-eight pounds!

But . . . I am doing much better. I have more room for others in my life and have found a wonderful woman that I feel so blessed to have in my life. I am a little bit gun-shy, and fears creep up that she too will leave, but I must not live my life in fear and will continue to do my best to enjoy each moment.

💔

19

Blindsided

Anna from Toronto, Ontario, Canada
36 years old
Separated two months

April 19, 2016, was the day when everything I knew to be true turned out to be false.

With our four year old sleeping on my lap, he turned to me and said, "I'm not OK, we're not OK, and I'm not happy." To say that I was blindsided would be an understatement. He had been acting distant and going out significantly more since February, but what happened between February and April I'll never know. How long had he been feeling that way? I don't know.

We had been together for ten years, married for five. In the bedroom, everything was great until I realized that for the last two months, I was the one initiating it all. When he married me, he took vows. So did I expect him to walk out on our marriage and family? Not one bit.

That morning, I had written him a letter that I never sent. It basically outlined that I knew something was wrong and that I hoped that it wasn't me and that I missed him and his affection. He had a tendency to fall into depression. He'd had two episodes while we were together, one while we were married, and was off work for eight months. I took care of him, never judged him, and though I had been a stay-at-home mom for years I got a job making lattes at the local coffee shop just to help out financially.

How did he hide all of this from me? We were inseparable and the best of friends, or so I thought. I asked him to leave that night. I couldn't breathe. There were no words to express the unbelievable amount of shock and sickness that took over me.

He came home two days later, saying that we had to make it work but that he was scared. He moped the entire weekend before leaving again on the Sunday evening. Now let me clarify: he wanted out of the marriage but refused to leave the house. He said the house was equally his (true) and that he would continue sleeping there. As for me, this was a method of kicking me while I was down. I needed time and space to process. I had just returned to work in February, so I had a new job while continuing to be my daughter's mother and coping with what just happened to our lives.

We are going into week eight. The change in him is mind-blowing. New clothes, new boxers, grew out his hair, going to the gym—and yet he still denies an affair. I saw him with the very girl who made me uncomfortable in the past, walking along the street. And then a co-worker said they saw them snuggling up together at a bar before our separation. He still denies it.

Now he sees me as an insecure psycho, and he said that's why he's leaving me. It's something new every week. On May 25, I came home to find separation papers on the counter. Before coming home that evening I had been at the doctor's, being told that I had tested positive for the lupus/ANCA gene. (Lupus and other auto-immune diseases run in my family.) I can promise you—that was rock bottom. I cried for hours. I thought about dying and how much easier that would be for me. I thought about how no one except for one person on his side had reached out to me. I thought about how no one would really care if I was gone—until I remembered her, my daughter, and how much pain that would cause her in her future.

Today is June 5th and we start mediation on the 8th. He looks different, he acts different— he's a complete stranger. I can't stand to talk to him because he is a shell of the person I fell in love with. Over the weeks, I've begged him to come home. He would never respond. I explained that this was a unilateral decision and that there are two people in a marriage and we should go to counselling. He won't go. He said he's done with me.

I don't understand. I don't know where we went wrong. I don't know how the love of my life, my prince, the father of my baby became this cold-hearted stranger. I think a lot . . . especially how he hadn't been single since his late teens. How he spent all his "party years" in relationships when most of us at the time were experiencing life and people. I've thought that he's going through a midlife crisis at the young age of 36. He puts significantly too much hair product in his hair and cruises around in his daddy's two-seater convertible Mercedes. It's absurd and slightly embarrassing when people tell me they've seen him.

I don't believe in divorce. The only way you could make me leave is through infidelity or physical abuse. I think people quit too easy. We live in such a disposable society, and for him to break his vows is the worst feeling I have ever had. The betrayal I feel is fierce. The anger and sadness and loss is destructive. Every waking minute hurts. Becoming another statistic in society disgusts me. The man I stood by through thick and thin turned his back on me and, without a second thought, walked out on our marriage.

I don't know where I stand. I don't know how I will survive. All I know is that however depressed I am, I have a responsibility to my daughter to continue to be the best mom ever. I hate him, but only because I love him. My daughter will forever have separate holidays because of him. The reality of my future is often unbearable.

One day at a time. Slow, deep breaths.

💔

20

You Don't Make Enough Money . . .

Susan from Lufkin, Texas, USA
62 years old
Separated four years

What a journey . . . one that I did not expect how hurtful one human being can be to another . . . after twenty-three years of marriage, two beautiful children . . . and then . . .

August 6, 2012, we pulled out of the driveway, on the way to work. Just a few houses down the block he looks at me, smiles, and says, "I got an apartment on the first and I will be moving all my things out." Stunned . . . I replied, "Excuse me?" He responded by saying, "Seriously." I calmly told him to "take me home . . . take me home now." He did . . . pulled the car in the driveway . . . and he went on to say, "You don't make enough money." He did not like my job. He was tired and burned out. I asked if there was anyone else. He said, "No, not yet." There were a very few words about counseling . . . and they were fruitless . . . he left . . .

My world came apart . . . tumbled to dust. His actions continued to be heartless and cruel. I wanted to die . . . even had a plan . . . but . . . my phone rang. I don't remember who it was, but . . . it stopped me. I would cry out in agony. I even scared one of my children. I could not sleep. I was a walking zombie . . . I did go to work . . . went through the motions . . . even tried to find him with an app for the cell phone. He found out and turned my phone off . . . "for the stunt." Yep, cruel . . . and I could continue to go on about what he said and what he did . . . and it was ugly and cruel. But . . . I found myself face to face with my children, who had been dealt horrible hurt as well.

I started doing research, reading, talking to friends, going to church . . . got into counseling. I learned that many people did not understand . . . told me to get over it . . . it hurt all over again. Then I took to heart what I was reading. . . . I was not alone. . . . This happens to many women . . . all over . . . not just at my house!! I found myself reaching out to the Healing Circle here in Texas, talked to several women, and have even become friends with one. Through counseling and reading I learned that it was not me . . . nothing I did or didn't do . . . it was all about him and his choices, his reasoning . . . or better said, his justifications . . . be them ever so wrong . . . he did it . . . he blamed me . . . he was ever so critical . . . so may lies . . .

My counselor suggested I start to journal, even write down his lies followed by the truth. Oh, there were many. She guided me through such a maze . . . and at the end . . . told me that when I was ready . . . to burn the journal. Closure . . . it hadn't afforded me any. . . . The day I burned the journal was beautiful . . . to watch all of those lies . . . those feelings . . . that time . . . just burn up and be gone.

What I do, and continue to do, is take time for me . . . learning what I like, who I am, what makes me happy, even learning to take a better care of myself. My children are college age . . . one has graduated and my youngest will next year. They are awesome people.

I will continue to grow . . . I have learned that I don't need to be in a relationship to be happy or fulfilled. I was brought up to think that . . . and it was something I learned that was not true . . . I have learned to enjoy my company, to go out by myself, or with a group, or even with another person . . . sometimes a date. As I continue to grow as a person, I have no doubt he did me a favor when he left.

21

Broken Open

Ann from Connecticut, USA
49 years old
Separated nine years

In November 2005, my then-husband met up with a woman through the website AshleyMadison.com. I, of course, would not know about this until much later. In fact, I only vaguely know of this specific date because of the unending sleuthing I did in an effort to understand what happened to my marriage. I still remember the day he told me, "This isn't working." Just like that, as if he was discussing an appliance or jigsaw puzzle piece. We were going back to my parents' home from his mother's house after sharing birthday cake for our oldest son's birthday in August 2007. He had just turned 11. I did in fact have to ask to what he was referring. "Our marriage," was his response. This news hit about one week before our fourteenth wedding anniversary.

Married fourteen years and together for two years of courtship, one of which we lived together. I felt like I had married a friend. We had a good foundation, and I truly trusted him in all ways. I would say that our marriage was without major conflict, even with common tripping points around money and sex and division of labor. So basically, we were squarely in the "norm" of married life. There were no addiction issues, no yelling or screaming, no visible fault lines in the marriage as seen by myself, or by others. Over the course of the few weeks following "the bomb," he denied the problems were connected to another person or persons. Lacking any other understanding of how the marriage had stopped working for him, I obsessed over trying to understand . . . any part of it. I got a trickle of truth over the next few weeks and months. "No one" became "a one-time thing" became "an acquaintance."

The crazy reached a peak on Christmas Eve 2007 while we were at his parents' home in another state. I found him in his father's office that evening and read on the computer screen over his shoulder, "It was nice waking up in your arms the other morning." That's all I remember reading, though I vaguely remember there was much more. He attempted to convince me that this was some kind of online virtual reality thing, but I was no longer buying the BS.

When we got home from that trip, I installed spyware on our family computer and almost immediately the facts and details poured forth. Stuff I remember in nightmares still but mostly can't put together in any sensible way during the waking hours. He moved out immediately after I got the TRUE truth. And so started the lost years. Time that I'm aware of but have little specific remembrance of other than chain-smoking during the day and multiple cocktails at night to get me to sleep. (I was never a smoker or a drinker . . . where did this come from?) So many weird and unkind conversations and events followed as I tried to keep some hope of reconciliation during the year-plus time frame leading up to the actual divorce.

I have come to learn, through Vikki's book and other offerings on marriage dissolution, that many abandoned wives experience similar conversations and events. The "I care about you but I don't love you," the "I deserve a trophy wife," the "I'd like to pick your future boyfriends." The drunken phone call from the mistress, the helpful therapist who shares in a couples' session that "You are acting like a victim."

Yes, I have learned that marriage therapists who don't know a thing about the wounds of unanticipated infidelity can harm more than they help. These particular experts charged $5,000 for an intensive marriage-repairing weekend. (Insert furious emoji.) Any of this sounds familiar? Years out from this period of time, do you still wake up in a sweat recalling painful details you have long since forgotten? I do. Though I will also say that seven years post-divorce (and nine years post–crazy time) the nightmares and triggers are MUCH less frequent.

Getting through the crazy and through the divorce was possible through the loving and sometimes brutally honest support of a few strong women in my life. One was a professional mentor who was able to let me "bleed out" the seemingly unending pain, to replay all the events as I struggled to find meaning, to question my sanity, and to question his sanity, all the while pointing me back to the idea that I would get through it.

Another important lifeline was a colleague who found herself in the exact same situation: her husband had an affair and bailed without anything that seemed to portend such behavior or departure. In those wee hours when the nightmares hit, she was the one I could call or text completely raw pain and know that she understood the crazy. I did the same for her. I wouldn't wish this on anyone, but it was a saving grace to know someone in the same circumstances.

The biggest challenge through those years were many other people, however well intended, who eventually got frustrated with the quicksand of emotions that come along when a spouse abandons the family. One thing I still feel sadness about is the fact that I exhausted a few good friendship because it just took so damn long to for me to stop hemorrhaging pain. In retrospect, I wish I could have exercised some restraint on my verbal diarrhea. I'm not sure that I could—the level of unexpected crazy is THAT intense. If you are reading this, I'm sure you are nodding your head in agreement.

I vividly remember the point when I finally let go of trying to understand and also let go of the need to have someone who has not experienced this kind of loss understand. It was one of those ridiculous post-divorce negotiations over some trivial matter concerning the children. (Actually, it was when he announced that he had plans to marry the skank and expected our boys to attend the ceremony.) In that moment, I realized that he would continue to have self-centered and questionable expectations of me and our sons, and that I (and they) do not have to do any more for him than what comfort dictates. I get to choose my actions, and the boys are also capable of making choices based on their comfort too.

Failure was never an option because I love my children too much to bail from their lives the way my former husband did. There are still days when the unfairness of the situation stings, mostly because I feel our boys got robbed. And on my worst days I still feel shame that many people know that my husband chose to leave me, and that some may have their ideas or judgments about the situation. (I live in a small town.) More often, however, I realize that good or bad, I am squarely in the driver's seat of my life. This path has painful terrain. No, it was NOT the "best thing" that ever happened to me, and I cringe when people suggest this. It WAS, however, a breaking open of my heart and soul that has made me a more mature, compassionate, and capable person: for that I am grateful.

22

Don't Let the Door Hit Your Butt on the Way Out!

C'iaran from Dublin, Ohio, USA
55 years old
Separated seven years

For three years, I watched my marriage go downhill because my husband had a female business partner who was blatantly chasing him. Her husband saw the writing on the wall and filed for divorce, which then gave her more time to spend with my husband. His narcissistic ego could not resist her hero worship, and I fell from his grace because I could not compete with someone who could play with him on the pool deck all day (they were swim coaches) because I have a day job. I even had him read the book *Not Just Friends* by Shirley Glass, about how affairs start, only to be told that my fears were unfounded and I just needed to get over my "jealousy."

As he slowly let her in and slowly kicked me out of his life, he started raging at me. Looking back, I believe he was trying to make it so bad that I would leave him first so he wouldn't have to be the bad guy. He would tell me he thought I was stupid. He got mad that he never got me to feel bad about myself, because by that point I really didn't care what he thought of me. I went to therapy to try to change me, only to be accused of going to therapy to try to get ideas from the therapist on how to manipulate him into changing.

My therapist recommended the book *The Verbally Abusive Man* by Patricia Evans. I read it and wrote out a contract for him to sign, outlining rules of how we would and wouldn't talk to each other. He refused to sign it. I think then he realized he was going to be held accountable for his inappropriate behavior and that I was not willing to accept the issues he was attempting to project onto me. The healthier I got, the unhealthier he became.

One night he told me that he needed to leave. It was not totally unexpected, and part of me was relieved. I had tried my hardest to make our marriage work, only to be continually told that I was not happy and that I was blaming him for it (totally not true because I know I am responsible for my own happiness). I knew that his leaving had nothing to do with me, but it had to do with him and his issues; and his issues would follow him into his relationship with his business partner. They say love is blind—she had watched him rage at me on more than one occasion, yet claimed never to have seen him treat me badly.

I asked him why he was leaving me, knowing he was moving into his business partner's house the minute he left. I expected to hear, "Because I'd rather be with . . ." What I was told is, "I'm leaving you because you are lying, manipulative, and controlling." I almost started to laugh because those were all projections of the parts of himself he denies. I told him he was being manipulated all right, but he was accusing the wrong woman of manipulating him. His business partner was so good at it; she was manipulating him and getting him to blame me for it. I asked him how he could think I'm smart enough to manipulate him if I'm as stupid as he claims I am. I saw the puzzled look in his eyes when I did not beg or plead with him to stay. He asked why I was letting him go, and I said because it's obvious it's what he's wanted for a long time.

My therapist said I would be devastated for about two weeks and then realize all my issues left with him, and that is what happened. His leaving was a gift. It was a blessing that allowed me the chance to re-create my life the way I wanted it to be. Events happen, and we assign the meaning. A divorce can be a tragedy or a blessing, and I chose to see it as a blessing.

I believe everything happens for a reason to further our soul's evolution. This was just part of my journey. My husband and I were clearly on different vibrational frequencies and, for some reason, I made him feel bad just by being me. I made a list of everything I wanted in a man so that the universe would know who to send my way when the time was right.

I asked friends and family to tell me what good they thought would come out of my husband leaving me. The best answer I got was from my friend Lars: "Never again will you have to compete with a narcissistic ego, a swim team, another woman, or a workout regimen. You will go on to find someone who is capable of truly loving you for the beautiful soul that you are, and you will both spend the rest of your lives in a happy, healthy relationship."

It took my ex almost a year to do the divorce paperwork and get it filed. He wanted to stay married for the tax break. He couldn't marry his partner because she'd lose her $57,000 a year in alimony. At the divorce hearing I told him, "I hope you are happy because this is what you want." He snarled at me and said, "This isn't what I want; this is what you want." Apparently he was OK with living indefinitely with another woman while staying married to me because it was a tax benefit to him. They even both work for the same Christian organization while continuing to live together unmarried.

At the suggestion of one of my ex-husband's old girlfriends, I threw a Dump the Chump party. It was supposed to be at our old hangout on Saturday night, but it got switched to Friday night at the last minute. My ex and his partner showed up, not knowing that was the party. They just thought I was hanging out with some people from work. When they went to leave, he said to me, "I hope you have fun at your party tomorrow night." I have no idea how he found out about it, but he was there and just didn't know it.

I believe living well is the best revenge. At the age of 48, I did not think I would get married again, but the Divine had other plans. Within a year I met and married a man who was everything on my list I asked for, and a few things that I didn't think to ask for. I have been happily married for six years to someone who wants to be married to me, and this marriage is so easy because there is no struggle to make it work. I trust he will never make a decision not in my best interest.

Sometimes the universe purges for us the people who are no longer in our best interest, but we refuse to let go of. If your marriage didn't work, that means there is something better in store for you.

23

'Til Death Do Us Part . . .

Grace from Bay Shore, New York, USA
59 years old
Separated four months

The day my son died, I wanted to hold his hand and go with him. The pain was . . . is . . . unbearable to lose a child, at any age. My beautiful son had suffered major traumas in his life and managed still to make a thriving career of music and was loved by so many he tried to help along his own path of struggle with addiction as his disease. He was my sunshine and my heartbeat, and after he had been in a coma for two weeks, I had to let him go. My husband had been by my side through everything, thirty-six years of marriage and many years of struggles with our two sons, and years leading to that moment of nightmarish hell, as many families of addicts can attest to. In my darkest hour, my deepest need of my husband, with full naïveté that he was still solidly in this now ultimate end to such heartache and desperation, I ached for any comfort, solace, or strength to bear this monumental pain. I needed my husband more than ever.

Something did not seem right. Even as I prayed endlessly over my son's bed, my husband seemed distracted—there, but not quite by my side as I wept and kept vigil. Once my son was set free, we went home together, but something was wrong. I cried alone. I was suddenly all alone and I felt it. My husband buried himself in "work" immediately following the service, flew away "on business" days after.

Just a few short weeks later, he announced that he would attend a small gathering of "professionals on a retreat"—would I mind? While he was away, alone, I tried to stand, to breathe, to think anything hopeful. After all my hopes, my only anchor had just been cut off at my son's death. When a child is sick, you are sick. A mother cannot think of her own life or pleasures while her child is in pain and suffering. My marriage was strained, of course, but had been through a war. Who was happy?

My husband said some things in that short time frame. He "wanted his life back." I said, "What life is that exactly? This IS our life. Yes, it is painful and challenging, but we have each other, and we have been already through so much. . ." There were some signs I was aware vaguely of, even in my grief. I was so lost in my sadness, yet the days he was away, I stood at my door, looking out at the peace of our home, and I felt a tiny thought take root.

I STILL had my husband. We STILL had time to make our life and our love into something beautiful, more so since we had weathered so much together and we had so much to keep us together, especially now, when we should carry forward between us our precious memories and keep our now more sacred bond ALIVE. A reason to live. My husband and I had a FUTURE we could now begin to imagine. Maybe changes. Maybe get help, and we will still have a life and love that brings healing and comfort. The gentle love of two people who have lost a war, lost a child, but survived.

As he walked up the path, home from his "conference," my heart swelled for the first time in a long time at the sight of him coming home to me. I had missed him. I needed and wanted him. All "men and women grieve differently" comments aside, I was ready to take his hand and begin to dream what things we had left to dream, together.

Just days later, he told me he was unhappy and had been for some time (the length matters not because it has changed many times since). I said, "Well, WHO has been happy?" "No, there was no one else," he said . . . but he was seeing a counselor. He would ask her. I said, "Ask HER? Ask her what? If you LOVE me? If you have to ask a stranger, there is a problem . . . and why would you go to ANYONE without me if it is a MARRIAGE relationship we have a problem with? She does not know me. How is she going to help us? Why didn't you say something when you realized?" "It was, is too late. I just need to know if I should stay if I am so unhappy. But there is no one else, and I still love you, OF COURSE," he said.

I have no words to describe the profound sense of abandonment, just days after the death of our son. I was beside myself in loss, grief, and disbelief that it was happening— that I was going to have to grapple with such a despicable act of desertion and immense insensitivity by my own husband, the father of my lost son, while still just in the first vast morass of deep grief. A mother loses a child; a husband, seemingly loving and supportive, at once decides he is done. He is unhappy, and overnight his wife becomes the source of his long unhappy life, deserving only of being left, and without a single tear or word to spare her already-broken heart.

I found the evidence—the receipts, the photos, the exchanged words, the new clothes, the rewritten history, the lies, the blame—all there. The "retreat"? He was in Cancun, bestowing gifts and all else one does in Cancun on holiday with a girlfriend. Yes, it had started before my son fell into a coma, while he struggled, we struggled, mired in the constant swirl of what addiction brings to everyone involved. His distraction in the hospital room? Texting, e-mailing, WHILE I CRIED and PRAYED over my dying son. He conducted his affair. He reached for HER, not me. SHE took part in it, knowing. Such a woman, a mother as well, I cannot imagine.

The husband I knew, he was dead. Whoever this was, is, I cannot understand, and no one else who knew us and cared can either. He had been a respectable man before; now he was a completely self-centered, cold-hearted being. I believe he could not handle the possibilities life holds; for better or for worse, in sickness and in health; he just wanted OUT and no reminders. So, he had to say it was my fault. The blame got bigger and bigger over a short time. I failed him, to assuage his own guilt. In his words, "There is not a single good thing I could say about you." "We had a good run," but he was "tired of taking care of you. I never should have married you. I was just trying to heal you."

Soon, these cold words turned into, "You abused me for years, neglected me, you don't even know me, and YOU are a narcissist." "I could explain more, but it would just hurt you." (!) "No blame." (!) Then, "If you don't agree to the lawyer I suggest, you are stupid and will end up in a trailer alone and broke." "Don't mess with me, you'll be sorry you did!" "You can't figure this out by yourself." My sorrow was stomped on. Seemingly overnight, my family was shattered. Even my surviving son is set aside by him, with just me to help him in his grief. My husband has a new life: "This one is yours," he said. His new life is all about what makes him happy. He is a completely altered person. I am left to hold everything together, all the broken pieces, alone.

He is HAPPY—"reborn!" His friends (a few new ones as unethical as he is) "respect [him] more now." Believe me, there is not a shred of love, respect, support, empathy, or common decency for me, or for my son. Did we have troubles? Yes. He was emotionally and mentally abusive for many years; we got counseling. I believed in my vows. He had control and anger issues that I lived with. After all, no one is perfect, not even me. I thought he loved me. I loved him. Everything else comes of that. This story is not about the details of his leaving; it is about WHEN he chose to do it. I have not met a person yet who can comprehend the timing. "It was coincidence," he says. Trauma breaks marriages, but WHO is HAPPY about it?

I bought the book *Runaway Husbands*. In it I found confirmation that I was not crazy, I was not alone, I was watching something play out that has happened before, and I could at least have that in my grief. I immediately knew he was not worth it; there was never any question of that. My SON, my SON, was my focus. I was determined to grieve him in the sacred way a mother must grieve and move through that.

If I resented my husband at all, it was for his interference in my grief process, for taking my attention away and requiring me to focus on the mess that he created. For making his own "happiness" more important than OUR marriage, than surviving, both of us, the worst thing parents could endure, as intact as possible, and maybe one day find some happiness, together, living around the common ground of our loss. Thirty-six years of a beautifully successful life, on the verge of a new era in which even I, in my loss, could see him clearly as the man I loved and wanted; in THIS time he took his leave.

It has only been a few months; we are already in the thick of divorce. Ugly, nasty, terrible divorce. For me, the issue of losing him pales to my deeper loss, and so in some blessed, impossibly sad way, my son's death helps me through it. In some equally but opposite twisted way, the divorce helps me through my grief. I am distracted by necessity to a certain degree, and that yanks me out of the darkest places I could go. God has a plan. I have substituted faith for the hope I lost when my son died. FAITH will get you there and reveal a beautiful thing that is yet to be seen. Let it go, let HIM go. Take my word for it: there are far more worthy places and people to put your love into. Anyone who can't value your life in their life is not worth grief. True love does not die. Ever. It's eternal. It endures all. It's magnetic. Love will find love again. Just be true to yourself, and love yourself. That's a first step forward.

24

Life Goes On

Shirley from Toronto, Ontario, Canada
65 years old
Separated one and a half years

Where to begin? We were married in 1971 and have three adult children. We were married forty years when thing started to change. My husband turned 60 and became chronically depressed. He was on and off medication for few years, but nothing seemed to help. He became more and more aggressive, critical, and judgmental of the children and myself. It wasn't easy, but I understood he had an illness and tried everything to ease his pain.

When he turned 64, he said he wanted a separation. He had met someone and wanted to pursue a relationship with this other woman. He left the house and moved into a basement apartment, but he continued this relationship with the other woman. He was back here two or three times a week, keeping tabs on the house and me. He just seemed too confused and undecided about his life. He said he still loved me and didn't know how things would work out.

Three months after he left, he and the girlfriend took a trip to Costa Rica for Valentine's Day. Again, more pain and devastation. Once they got back from their trip, he dropped by the house one day to say that he didn't see why he had to live in an apartment and pay rent when he had a perfectly good house to live in and announced he was moving back into the house, although in the basement, where a bedroom was set up. So, he did, and he continued his weekend trips away with the girlfriend. I just haven't the words to express how painful this period of my life was. I was living in a constant daze, a continuous state of confusion and pain.

While he was living in the basement, we started to reconcile. One afternoon, I was working in my office at home and he came in and started crying. He said he was confused, didn't know what he wanted, and couldn't go on like this. I told him to make a decision because I couldn't go on living under the same roof with him while still loving him the way I do.

A day later he said he had made his decision. He chose to move out and be with the girlfriend. He spent the next day or two packing his things, while I tried to continue working and ignoring my emotional state. As far as I was concerned, he had made his choice and it was finally over.

He had his car loaded up and was about to leave. I heard him come into the house and I thought he was coming to say good-bye. Instead, he broke down, started weeping again, and said he couldn't imagine a life without me, that he wanted to stay if I could forgive him and take him back once and for all. I did.

Worst mistake of my life!

We had a wonderful year of reconciliation, weekend trips away to lovely hotels, resorts, theatre, Sunday afternoon drives, all very romantic and loving. He was turning 65 that year, retiring, and we were planning our retirement years. We had no debt and were looking forward to traveling and spending time together. As part of his retirement plan, he was going to teach English to Spanish students, so he was learning Spanish.

To expedite the process, he decided that a three-month immersion course in Spanish would be a good thing, so he checked out Spanish schools and decided on one in Ecuador. He was due to leave for the Spanish school on September 17, 2014. Our birthdays were September 12 and 15, and we wanted to do something special. So, we spent a week in the honeymoon cottage of our favourite resort and had a wonderful time together.

He left for Ecuador on September 17. We wrote to each other every day—beautiful, romantic love letters. By November, I started noticing a change in his e-mails. He was due back on December 11, and I was counting the days. I asked him what was going on and noted that his e-mails were sounding more distant and almost terse. On November 17, he sent a long missive explaining that the marriage was over, he wanted a partner who would share his passion for South America, and that we have led separate lives for a long time.

He said life was too short, that he had things he wanted to do without feeling guilty, that he had raised his family and that chapter of his life was over and now it was his time. I can't tell you how that felt, that I was a chapter in his life. Once again, devastation and heartache you wouldn't believe, actual physical pain. I could literally feel my heart breaking. We had, I thought, rebuilt our relationship after his affair and were looking forward to our retirement years together.

Fast-forward to today.

It's been an awful journey, getting from there to here. Some days are completely hopeless and I find no reason to live, that I'm a waste of space. I feel I have nothing to offer anyone. He was the only man I ever loved and trusted with my life. Not being wanted by my own husband has left me with little or no self-worth. I've gone through every emotion imaginable, and still do, from anger, constant sadness, suicidal thoughts, loneliness, despair, to even still loving the man, although I know the man I loved is long gone.

He is now divorcing me and forcing me out of my home. Ours was a traditional marriage: I was a stay-at-home mom, working part-time to supplement the family income, but I have no pension of my own. I will be taking a lump sum pension payment in lieu of his portion of the house. I don't want to leave my home, but I have no choice. I love my neighbourhood and my neighbours. But, once again, I have no choice in the matter and my life is still being controlled by this man I called my husband for so many years.

In hindsight, I see how that last year he spent with me was part of a plan. He turned 65 that final year, spent the year sorting out his pensions and planning his life in Ecuador without me. He refuses to share the pension until we're divorced. So, in essence, he absconded with all our retirement money and pensions. I've had to continue working, doing typing from home, to make ends meet. It's been a struggle financially, while he's happily retired and travelling the world.

This, more than anything else, has opened my eyes to the kind of man he really is—not the one I thought he was. This is anger! I no longer feel any love for him and actually see light at the end of my long tunnel. There are days now where I'm actually happy and don't give him a second thought. I will survive. I will find a place to live, make a home for myself, and just get on with it. I have no other choice. I've been to hell and back and am stronger for it.

Ladies, please remember that you are worth more than what you believe, that there is light at the end of the tunnel, and never give up on yourself!

25

Freedom

Daniela from Brisbane, Australia
45 years old
Separated three years

Although I work as a psychiatrist, nothing ever prepared me for the emotional devastation of my own husband admitting he was in love with our son's music teacher, followed by his departure two weeks later. Usual story—she was younger, needier, adoring, and flirtatious. Sure, I'd seen many patients who had presented in distress following relationship breakups, knew it was an incredibly difficult experience, and felt sorry for them. But going through it myself gave me a much deeper understanding of the huge hurt caused by infidelity to both partners and children, in addition to the awkward adjustment to being a single mum in a world that seems full of happy, intact families.

The moment my ex-husband told me he was leaving is permanently burned on my memory, although the days and weeks that followed are a painful, confused blur. He had been irritable and cold for months, repeatedly denying that anything was wrong. Looking back, I now marvel at the power of denial as a defence mechanism. I had all the classic red flags; for example, the previously chatty teacher was visibly uncomfortable talking to me, my workaholic husband was leaving work early to pick my son up from her lessons, and he started his own lessons with her—sometimes on Saturday nights, for hours!

He moved into the spare room, claiming he couldn't sleep . . . and so on. I clearly recall Googling "signs your husband is having an affair," answering yes to every sign, and closing my laptop with a sick feeling in my stomach. Then blocking it out. So it really shouldn't have been a surprise when I finally demanded the truth from him. My husband of eighteen years was slowly suffocating our marriage through his cowardly dishonesty, while siphoning money away to rescue his princess and her children.

In retrospect our marriage was not healthy; we frequently clashed over my husband's tendency to pick up extra work or teaching duties on the weekends I was rostered on duty, or to abandon holidays midway to return to tackle paperwork. His response was always the same: "Tell them you're married to a busy surgeon." He had always been the more ambitious and dominant partner, and in retrospect he had been drawn to the shyer and more dependent person I had been many years before.

I also look back and see narcissistic traits in him that grew over the years, an occupational hazard of his profession. However, I have many irritating flaws too, and had decided we could still make this work, given that marriage requires compromise. What I didn't learn till later was that he'd tired of me long ago and had been looking for a replacement for years, facts he shared with me before moving out. Details like that made me doubt the whole history of our relationship and question what really happened.

It took the best part of two years to get anywhere near normality for me. What shook me the most was the physical pain of heartbreak, and the exhausting months of tears, poor sleep, and no appetite. I felt like my chest had been ripped open and my heart stabbed with a knife. My memory and concentration were seriously impaired; I felt like I'd lost half my brain early on, and it takes a long time to recover from something like that. I was also frightened by the intensity of the anger in the early months and could understand, if not condone, why abandoned partners react violently. The punching bag in our garage was a good outlet for that, as was rehearsing with my psychologist how I would deal with seeing the teacher. When I eventually came face-to-face with her at the shops, I was able to walk past her and bite my tongue, as planned.

Several things were particularly helpful to cope with the stress of separation, moving houses, and my children's unhappiness in trying to adjust to the instant stepfamily. Reading books like *Runaway Husbands* and divorce support websites were incredibly reassuring. Rather than run *away* from the pain by using pills or alcohol, I ran *with* it to cope—training for and completing a marathon that same year, which had been a long-term goal of mine. When my running injuries put that outlet on hold, I turned to meditation and am grateful for that too, as previously it had been something I put off because I was too busy or too impatient.

Counselling with a wise older psychologist was also helpful; he talked a lot about this being more about my ex-husband's issues, rather than flaws in myself, and encouraged me to rebuild my life. Early on I also spoke with women who had been through the same years before. Some had remarried and some hadn't, but they all told me that my children and I would get through this OK, and someday I would see that I deserved better than my ex. I try to repay that now for people going through the same.

I have learned some important lessons: the value of loyal friends, family (including my supportive in-laws), and colleagues, and the strength of independence. I miss the big extended-family dinners, the couples' dinner parties, and the comfort of lying curled up in bed with someone whom you thought loved you the way you were. My best friends let me rant and cry; others made unhelpful comments like "The pathology in marriages is fifty-fifty"; and others were so shocked and unsure how to react that they literally backed away mid-conversation and avoided me in future.

So three years on, I can genuinely say I would not undo what happened now, although I cannot forget the hurt my children went through. I have been freed from a man who did not respect me or treat me as an equal, and probably had been unfaithful before. I feel a lot wiser about human nature and relationships, and better able to tolerate uncomfortable emotions. In trying to understand what happened to my husband, I mentally retraced his steps, which led me to the edge of a pit, the one where you contemplate your hectic life and endless obligations, with a looming awareness of passing youth and mortality. At that point, my ex ran away with his young mistress, probably with no conscious awareness of these issues. I've talked over these themes many times with friends; by the third anniversary of him dropping his bombshell, I just felt genuine relief that I was divorced and have my freedom.

My main challenges now are learning to co-parent and keep my boundaries, and learning to trust again so I might have a relationship in the future. Many of my friends who separated at the same time re-partnered quickly and suggest that it's time to think about dating. However, I'm not particularly interested and would rather work on being happily self-sufficient first, so that if a relationship happens it's a bonus. More importantly, my kids need one "good enough" parent who is there for them in their teen years, and that's my main role for now.

26

A Real Heartbreaker

Tamara from Tulsa, Oklahoma, USA
44 years old
Separated one year

"Massive heart attack. You are having a massive heart attack, and we are life-flighting you to the hospital." That can't be, I thought. I'm only 43 and in good health. Those are words I will never forget.

Just five days earlier, I was enjoying a family vacation with my spouse of twenty-one years and our three beautiful children, celebrating our oldest turning 13 with a trip to New York City. While we were getting dressed to start our tour of the Empire State Building, my 7-year-old daughter was playing a game on Dad's phone. Frustrated with a stream of text messages that kept coming through and interrupting her game, she blurted out, "Argh! I wish Dad's girlfriend would quit texting him! She is messing up my game!" Shocked, I asked her to repeat that. Her dad laughed it off, saying she has such a funny sense of humor. My daughter said, "It's OK, Mom. All the kids in second grade like more than one boy or girl."

I wasn't sure if it was a joke or not. I couldn't imagine my spouse having an affair. Not. At. All! We had been together for twenty-five years, since I was 18 and he 21, and married for twenty-one years. By all accounts, we were the ideal, happily married couple. He was a deacon at church, adult Sunday school Bible teacher, occasional preacher, and had even baptized our children. He would always tell me that I never had to worry about him straying because he "was accountable to God" and he was "more afraid of consequences from God" for such sins. He has even (just a few weeks earlier) counseled a neighbor who was going through an unexpected divorce. There was no way this God-fearing man who always endearingly called me his "bride" would cheat.

Nevertheless, I could not shake the feeling that something was wrong after my daughter had said that. So, I snuck the cell phone away for a few discrete minutes. What I discovered ripped me to the core. He had been texting clearly inappropriate messages to a woman who did contract work for his office—messages of "I love you," "I can't wait to be in your arms again," and "It moves me so much when I see you read your Bible." Yeah, that last one was not lost on me at all. I didn't know if this was sexual or not at this point. All I knew is that I didn't want to cause a scene on my daughter's 13th birthday and our special trip. I sucked it up and waited until two days later to confront him.

When I asked him about why he was so secretive about his phone, he denied, denied, denied. I had to fully confront him with what I had seen. Then, he went full Jekyll and Hyde on me. This loving man I had known for two decades blasted me with news he was having a sexual and emotional affair and that he "deserved to be happy." He yelled at me, accusing me of a variety of wrongs that I had never once— not once!—ever heard from him, in which he detailed everything I did that annoyed him or otherwise made him unhappy. Everything he said from that point on was based on half-truths and complete misrepresentations. Somehow he had created this false reality and re-written our love story in his mind to justify what he had done.

The next day the kids and I went to stay at my parents so I could think and pray about what I should do. I was so heartbroken, so overcome with grief like I'd never known. I did not know this man. Who was he? And what did he do with my husband? I cried for five days straight, overcome with grief, a sense of abandonment and loss. Then, on day five, I awoke with a tight chest and pain in my left arm. I began vomiting and my parents drove me straight to the ER. That's when I was life-flighted, having suffered a massive heart attack.

Known as broken heart syndrome, a massive heart attack caused by deep grief almost took my life. The doctors said this phenomenon is typically seen in widows and widowers who die within days of each other—overcome with grief at the loss of a decades-long spouse. I too had just experienced such deep grief from the breakdown of a two-decades-long marriage.

Even after this heart attack, my spouse still continued to treat me with utmost contempt—unlike anything I had ever seen in him. He stayed in the house with me until we could go to counseling and decide what to do. I had a second massive heart attack just a week later.

About a month after my recovering from two heart attacks, we began marriage counseling and worked on restoration and reconciliation. I believed it had worked, and we spent the next eleven months rebuilding trust, working on forgiveness, and dating again—starting anew. I put 110% into everything he felt I needed to work on. I did absolutely everything I could to make him happy and feel loved. I wanted this marriage to work and wanted our kids to have a solid family.

Just eleven months later, on Valentine's Day, he talked in his sleep, mumbling, "I know our kids will get along great with [his affair partner's name]'s kids." I woke him up and asked him why he said her name. He denied, denied, denied. He swore, "I love you baby! I wouldn't do that to you! I swear I haven't talked to her in a year!" Although he fell right back to sleep, I just couldn't. I couldn't shake the gut feeling that something was wrong.

I checked his phone in the wee hours that night, which I hadn't done in several weeks. He apparently was very good at deleting messages and voice mails. I was able to locate the deleted messages and calls and saw they were still communicating. He had straight up lied to me. I immediately woke him up and asked when this had started. He denied it again. Told me I was crazy. Once he realized I had seen the messages, he pulled his Jekyll/Hyde act again and went insane— yelling at me and telling he was so unhappy. He said, "I am so sick of you being sick and having to take care of you!" (Never mind that he caused the heart attack.) He said, "I took a bite of the apple and I liked it. We are done. I choose her. She makes me happy. And I deserve to be happy." And just like that, it was over and he moved out the next day.

This was so hard for me and the kids to accept because just the day before he was hugging and kissing me and telling me he loved me. He had been very physically and verbally demonstratively affectionate towards me. It confused the kids greatly. In fact, my 11 year old said, "Dad, I don't understand why you are leaving. You kiss Mom and tell her you love her all the time." That's how crazy this was to us all. One minute affectionate and loving and the next, "We're done." He even admitted that I had addressed every area about me he had complained about in counseling (whether I believed they were true or not). But he claimed, "You were just manipulating me."

As much as I wanted and still want to fight for our marriage, I now realize that there is nothing left for me to do. The problem is not me. It never was. From a spiritual perspective, I see him as a prodigal son. I feel God has told me this is no longer my battle but His. Only time will tell if the prodigal will return. I don't know that I will still be here waiting for him. I cling to God's promise that He can make beauty from ashes and make all things new. I interpret that for myself personally, He is transforming me into a better person and for me to rise above Jekyll/Hyde.

I have not engaged in hateful, spiteful comments. I don't think it's productive. I constantly remind myself that he is my kids' father. I don't have to be married to him, but he will always be their dad. Our divorce is still pending, but he has clearly moved on to this other woman (who was also married with kids). I look at my daughters and think I want to be an example to them that they don't deserve to be treated like this and that they are strong enough to stand on their own.

I realize now that although I almost died from heartbreak, I'm actually stronger than I realized. I'm not the one who died. The man I married is dead. Someone I don't know or recognize now lives in his body. I've been coming to grips with this part of my story slowly but surely. It's only been four months since he left us. My best friend and I are holding a funeral for the man I married in July on my twenty-second anniversary date. We will eulogize that extraordinary man I loved for more than twenty-five years, the one who always called me his bride, the love of his life. We will rejoice in the wonderful memories I had with him. I don't know what happened to him, but that man is gone. I look forward to healing and mending the shattered pieces of my heart.

💔

27

How I Survived
Eighteen Months of Hell

kathi from Naples, Florida, USA
63 years old
Separated eleven years

There is no way I can tell my story in 1,200 words! Even after all this time (I have been divorced since March 2007), recalling the Eighteen Months of Hell it took to divorce the lying, cheating coward is painful and makes my stomach churn. So I will limit my remarks to the things that helped me most through that terrible period in my life.

HOW TO SURVIVE AN UNWANTED DIVORCE

1. Retain your own legal counsel.

The first step in this process is to EDUCATE YOURSELF on divorce law in your state. A great resource can be found at www.divorce-source.com. Once you are armed with this basic information, start looking for a reputable attorney who specializes in family law *and* who is willing to go to trial, if necessary, to get you the best possible financial settlement. DO NOT let your runaway husband pull the wool over your eyes and lull you into believing that he is going to be FAIR. And no matter what he promises, DO NOT use the same attorney he does! From the day they tell you they are leaving (or the day you discover that they have left), they will do their best to confuse you and/or lull you into a state of complacency while they liquidate assets and start to squeeze you financially.

Remember: If his lips are moving, he is LYING!

2. Find a qualified counselor or licensed therapist.

To this day, I owe my sanity to the amazing therapist I saw at least weekly through the entire Eighteen Months of Hell. Her professional services weren't cheap, but you can't put a price on your own mental health! There is no doubt in my mind that if it weren't for her (and my attorney), I would either be living in a cardboard box or doing ninety-nine years to life on two counts of homicide (the now X and the Other Woman).

3. Invoke the "no contact" rule.

Trust me when I tell you that seeing, talking to, or even e-mailing with a runaway husband will only leave you feeling worse than you already do. The simple fact of the matter is that he disengaged emotionally from you long before you had a clue he was planning to leave you. At this point, he no longer has YOUR best interests at heart, and while he may tell you what you want to hear, he has no intention of following through.

4. Take good care of yourself.

I can't stress this enough! While you may have trouble dragging yourself out of bed each day, you MUST keep moving. Two months after the Day of Devastation, I caught a glimpse of myself in the mirror and barely recognized the person looking back at me. I was thin to begin with—but when I stepped on the scale, I was shocked to see that I had lost fifteen pounds that I didn't have to lose. I looked much older than my 52 years, and my clothes hung off me like a scarecrow. I hadn't slept more than a few hours at a time and I had no appetite whatsoever. Not good!

Then, when I learned that the runaway husband had been having an affair, I made an appointment with my gynecologist to be tested for STDs. Lucky for me, I was in the clear, but it was very scary to think that he had risked my health as well as broken my heart. I also talked with my internist, and together we decided that I needed to get on some antianxiety meds for the short term. Self-care is of utmost importance during this time of your life!

5. Surround yourself with true blue friends.

Don't be surprised when those you THOUGHT were true friends turn their backs or bury their heads in the sand. When a long-term marriage breaks up, it makes everyone feel insecure. I was shocked and disappointed with quite a few people's reaction to the news that my marriage was ending—they simply disappeared. But I was equally surprised at the number of good folks who popped out of the woodwork to comfort and help me through this awful time.

6. Find a support group.

Just a few months into the process, someone told me about DivorceCare. This is a most helpful program, usually run under the auspices of a local church, that meets weekly for twelve-week sessions. To find a DivorceCare group in your area, go to www.DivorceCare. org. There is strength in numbers, and when you are part of a group that is going through the same horrible life change, you will no longer feel alone. You might also find a similar support group through Meetup.com. AND one group that I discovered eighteen months AFTER my divorce was final is www.DailyStrength.org. They offer an online support group for nearly every physical and emotional aspect of being human, with lots of helpful links to books and websites that provide insight, experience, and tools for surviving divorce.

7. Keep a journal.

I have kept journals since 1972 but was shocked when I realized that my last entries had been in 1988, with just a few pages written in the seventeen years since we had bought our little farm. During the Eighteen Months of Hell, I filled thirteen college-ruled spiral notebooks with my thoughts, feelings, and discoveries. When I would review those new entries periodically, I could measure my emotional progress and it helped me tremendously.

8. Remember: Now is not forever.

While it may seem that this nightmare may never end, you have to remind yourself that this, too, shall pass. I wrote that phrase on sticky notes and put them all over my house and in my car so that I wouldn't forget!

9. Accept your new reality.

This is, perhaps, the most difficult step in the journey. I was the epitome of the Queen of Denial for nine long months in the process. I still expected my husband to realize that he had made a big mistake and come back to the marriage, and until a certain point, I would have taken him back and given him another chance. It wasn't until my sister pointed out to me that I had been ALONE IN THE MARRIAGE for a very long time that I began to ACCEPT the fact that my marriage was over and could not be restored. Not a happy realization, but it was a DEFINING MOMENT for me and a huge step toward healing and moving on.

10. Start building a new life for yourself.

Focus on the positive aspects of your life, and think of all the things you have always wanted to do but had put on the back burner for your marriage and raising a family. Take a class at your local community college or online. Get involved in volunteer work or start focusing on where you want to be career-wise and take steps to attain your goals. These steps will also open you up to meeting new people and getting out of your house! It's far too easy to sit home and feel powerless. PUSH YOURSELF if you have to, but you will feel a whole lot better than if you stayed at home feeling sorry for yourself.

28

Hurt

Meredith from Hudson, Ohio, USA
43 years old
Separated five years

My story truly began in 2009, which lead to my husband leaving me and our two boys in July 2011, resulting in divorce in 2013. It was much more than heartbreak; it was complete devastation. In 2009, two of my husband's friends ended their marriages and my husband began spending more time with these two friends, which I chalked up to him being a good friend. That Christmas one of those friends spent the holiday with our family so he wouldn't have to be in his new home alone. My husband seemed distant, but every time I asked how he was or what was going on, he'd always tell me it was his new job, which wasn't what he thought it would be.

At this time, I also noticed I was receiving calls from 1-800 numbers asking about missed payments on various expenses. My husband handled all the family finances, and when I asked him about the calls he'd always tell me that the payment was late but it was made. Ignorance is truly bliss because as a stay-at-home mom, I bought groceries as needed, all the utilities were on and we had a roof over our heads, so I assumed all was well; I couldn't have been more wrong.

After about a year and a half of fielding these calls, I took the ultimate, fateful call in June of 2011. It was the mortgage company telling me that our mortgage was three months past due and foreclosure proceedings had begun. I confronted my husband over the phone and he simply said he just got behind, don't worry. Then I suggested we withdraw from an annuity, which he'd arranged for me from a pension I had when I was working full time, to at least catch up the mortgage. He was dismissive regarding the annuity so I scoured the house looking for any information I could on it. I called the general customer service number at the bank, and the man on the other end of the phone told me that the annuity had been cashed out in October of 2009 and the account was closed.

There are no words to accurately describe what I was feeling. I called my husband, who was out of town for work, and asked him who needed the money. He told me I'd get the money back, but he wouldn't answer my question. The next day he came home and we sat our two boys down at the kitchen table for lunch. We went upstairs to our room, and I asked him to explain to me what was going on. It was only at this time that he informed me that "It's more than the money; our marriage has been bad for a while." I went into sheer panic mode. I asked him what that meant, and he would just repeat himself.

From that point on, I gathered and hid every piece of mail; he began staying out more and talked to me even less than before. I dug in, trying to figure out if he was going through a midlife crisis and how to get our finances back on track. What I knew about was just the beginning of the financial nightmare. Not only did he steal the only savings we had (my annuity), he also ran up credit cards that were in my name by transferring balances from one card to another. He was having the statements sent to his work e-mail address. I begged him to help me figure things out, but he wouldn't.

Then I received his work cell phone bill in the mail. I actually debated with myself over whether to open it. I had never invaded my husband's privacy before. Ultimately, I decided to open it, and it was literally sixty-eight pages of calls and texts to the same number. I called the number; a woman (I later learned she's twelve years younger than him) answered. I said, "Hello." She said, "Hello, who is this?" I said, "I was just calling to see who was spending so much time with my husband." She paused and hung up. I took that as confirmation.

At this point, even though I knew I'd been lied to, stolen from, and now cheated on, I still wanted him. Just because he didn't love me, which was clear from the secrets he'd been keeping, didn't mean my love for him had stopped. I'm sure I would have been miserable keeping all those secrets, but even though I was willing to forgive and get things right again, because I had clearly failed him somehow, but all he would say was, "I just don't think it'll get better." When I confronted him about her, he of course denied the relationship—and the day the boys returned from visiting my family, he was gone. It took me three days to realize that he wasn't coming home.

Hysterically, I ran to my friend and neighbor, who had been through a divorce, begging for help. Her advice to me was to file for at least a legal separation. She explained to me that she filed for divorce three times before she actually followed through with it, but in my case she said, "You're a stay-at-home mom with no income. You don't know where he is and he isn't returning calls, texts or e-mails, so it's time for mama bear to take over and take care of the boys."

I have been so consumed over the years with getting the finances back on track, finding a job, and taking care of our boys that it's just now hit me that it's time to mend my heart. I'll never be married again, and that's a conscious choice. The financial devastation was way too much, and I don't think I'll ever be able to allow anyone to get that close to me again. Once was enough of that kind of betrayal and hurt. I now choose to raise our boys how we intended from the beginning; I just now accept that he no longer wants to be part of our life.

The hardest part right now is that he has a daughter with the person he betrayed our boys and me with, and he tries to bring her and the daughter to our boys' events and activities. I find it cruel, hurtful, and distasteful to expect us to have to see the three of them together during the only moments when our boys have their mom and dad in the same place. He unilaterally decided that our only communication of any kind is via e-mail. I feel it's simply because he does not want to answer my questions or accept ownership of the nightmare he created for our boys and me.

29

Why?

Julie from Nottingham, England, UK
51 years old
Separated fifteen years

I met my husband in 1986, when I was a student teacher at university. He was eight years older and a successful businessman. He literally swept me off my feet. He took me to places I could never dream of going and treated me like a princess.

We got married in 1988 and went on to have three beautiful children—a son and two daughters. He was a fantastic dad, very hands-on, and he doted on his children. I could trust him completely to look after them, and he was very involved in school life and all the activities they did. He was the manager of our son's football team and took the girls to ice skating and ballet lessons.

We spent a few years living in Saudi Arabia and saved hard to buy a holiday home in Koh Samui, Thailand. Finally we came home and settled in a beautiful little village. Our son went to private school and the girls went to the local school. They were doing really well and we were happy.

I paint the picture of an idyllic marriage, and maybe I look back through rose-coloured glasses, but we weren't the kind of people to argue and were just busy doing everything we could for our family. Looking back at this time, I think that maybe we had become too engrossed in the children and had lost our relationship. We didn't really go out much as a couple and sometimes we didn't communicate as much as we could, but we would snuggle up and watch television in the evenings with a bottle of wine.

In March 2001, my husband surprised me with a trip to Paris for our anniversary. There was no expense spared. We ran around Paris like teenagers, laughing and carefree, as we didn't have the children. It was a beautiful weekend, with not a hint that anything was wrong or about to change.

At the end of March, I came home from work and the children, who were 11, 7, and 3, were home alone. They hadn't seen Daddy and didn't know where he was. I ran upstairs and saw that his clothes were gone, along with some belongings. I panicked and tried to ring him, but there was no reply. I remember feeling sick with worry but somehow knew I didn't need to ring the hospitals, police, etc. Deep down I knew where he had gone.

The next day I rang our house in Thailand, and he was there. He said he needed space to think and didn't know when he would be coming back. He wouldn't talk to me about money, plans, or the children. He simply didn't want to know and made me feel like it was my fault that he needed time to sort his head out. I went into super-mum mode. I was determined that nothing would change for the children. They still went to all their activities, and I carried on working full time as a teacher. Looking back I just don't know how I did it.

At Christmas, he came back for what he wanted to be a perfect family Christmas and he bought expensive gifts for the children. He had been gone for nine months, and the atmosphere in the house was scary. He wouldn't look me in the eye and he wouldn't talk about what he was doing or the future. When I went upstairs, he went downstairs. I knew as he was leaving to get back to the airport that we wouldn't see him again, and I was right. I often wonder why I didn't fight. Why did I just let him walk out that day? Could I have said or done something different? Why weren't we good enough? What had we done to deserve this?

In 2002, he stopped giving me my money and I had to find a new school for my son and sell my beautiful family home. There were times when we had no money and I didn't know how we were even going to eat from day to day. I found a new house and the children settled down into their new lives without Dad, and we became a unit. I made sure that I never rubbished their Dad in front of them, and if he ever did ring or contact the children I always let them have that contact. To me it was so important that they had their relationship with their Dad and made their own minds up about him. It wasn't many years before they gave up on him altogether.

In 2006, I began to get ill. I was run down and so tired. I had recurrent kidney infections and also had to have a hysterectomy. I spent weeks in and out of hospital, and mentally I was just exhausted. It was around that time that I began to self-harm. I hated myself. I was alone, sad, fat, and ugly, and my husband had abandoned me and moved across the world to get away from me without ever telling me why. I knew why in my head—it was because I was stupid, disgusting, pathetic, and a bad person. I started taking antidepressants and they helped for a while.

My children were my life and were all very successful, and when my eldest daughter went to university in 2011, my world fell apart. I couldn't handle two children leaving home and struggled to find a purpose. I had always been so busy that I had lost me. Eventually I tried to hang myself and ended up in a psychiatric hospital for three months. They diagnosed me with PTSD following the trauma of being abandoned. It was something that I had never talked about, and it haunted me. I had nightmares where I tried to run after my husband but my legs wouldn't work and my body was heavy. I used to wake up crying and shaking and would just curl up on the bedroom floor.

I began to have therapy and to try to widen my circle of friends and the activities that I did for me. It was important that I wasn't just a mum and an abandoned wife. I had lost my identity, and I found it hard to trust people and to let others help me. I thought that I was weak if I did that. Eventually I got stronger, and talking to others and letting them in helped so much.

Now my children are 27, 24, and 20. My son is in a relationship and has his own house. He has a good job and is settled. I have a good relationship with him. My eldest daughter lives with her boyfriend and also has a good job. She is my best friend and a joy in my life. My youngest daughter has just come back from studying at university in America. I am so proud of her, as she is my baby and never really had her dad in her life.

My children make me proud, and I stand tall knowing that I did my best for them. Their dad lost out on so much and it's a shame he will never know the wonderful adults they have become.

I am not mad, sad, fat, unlovable, or any of the things I used to tell myself. What happened was not my fault and I didn't deserve it. I think it's a shame that my marriage wasn't what I thought it was and it hurt, but I am stronger and looking forward to my future with my wonderful family.

30

August 10

Cory from San Antonio, Texas, USA
45 years old
Separated five years

August 10. This is a significant date for me. August 10, 2000. This date was one of the happiest days of my life. We brought our son home from the hospital that day. I don't think I need to describe to anyone why that date has meaning for me.

August 10, 2010. Ten years later. To the day.

I came home from a trip to visit my parents. My son was not with me—he'd stayed with my parents for an extra week. My loving husband picked me up at the airport. He told me how much he missed me. He told me a funny story about a mishap with the electrical system at the house. We went for lunch. We held hands. It was good to be home.

Once home I unpacked my suitcase on our bed. We had just bought a $3,000 dollar bedroom set a few months prior. In fact, the mirror to the set had yet to be hung up on the wall. It was a beautiful furniture set that went perfectly in our dream house. Our happy house . . . and then I found her shirt between the mattress and the footboard.

He told me it was my shirt. He told me it wasn't an affair. They were just friends. He told me they just went to the lake together with a few other people and she just changed in our bedroom. Even though we lived in a 4,000-square-foot home with multiple bathrooms and bedrooms, she was in my bedroom.

I told him I believed him, that he was not that guy who has affairs.

That I knew he loved me and I knew that he loved our family. He stayed at the lake for the next week to figure things out. It was the first time I heard that he "was unhappy for years." It was the first time he said he lied that "he lit up when I walked into the room," he just said that because . . . well, I don't know why he said that. Why would someone make that up? He told me he would not walk out on our family.

He left three months later, a few weeks before my 40th birthday. We had been married for thirteen years. He said he would be fair. But then he told me during divorce negotiations that he would lie about money just to not have to pay the correct amount of money during the split of our finances. He said he did not want any visitation with our son. He would only want visitation for his parents. WHAT? He told me he would not get into a custody battle with me. Then he helped his parents sue me for additional visitation.

And then, he married her. He didn't include his only child in the wedding or even tell his son about the marriage until months after. Who does that? It was all unbelievable. I couldn't eat. I couldn't sleep. He was "businesslike" with e-mails. Almost sounding lawyerly. Yet he was no lawyer.

I was the sole supporter during the marriage, going back to work when our son was four weeks old. There was no spousal support. And now, five years later, all the communication I get is related to how much he is paying in child support. He thinks I have gotten too much. I think I have lost everything. He pays the minimum child support the law allows and he will not assist with ANYTHING extra.

This from a guy who coached soccer for his son's team. Who never missed a game. Who was home every night. Who wanted our son to have everything he had as a child. Who told me I was his trophy wife. Who told me how proud he was that I worked so hard for our family. It was, the only word that comes to mind is, unbelievable.

He told me he was leaving because he wasn't having fun. He told me I was a difficult person. He told me he was leaving because our son and I were not making him any money. Again, I was the sole supporter for most of the marriage. Nothing made sense. He said he didn't like the underwear I wore. Who says that??? (P.S., I wore matching sets, not granny panties—thank you very much.)

He left to be with a woman who was older than I am, I assume. She has a son a decade older than our own. She was a secretary. So assuming no education. (No dig to secretaries here, but he was leaving me when I was making 80K to go with a woman who was making maybe 30–40K . . . and telling me that what I brought home wasn't enough.) It made no sense. I had had met her previously. She made no impression on me. And he told me his friends and business partners said I was hot, and the few times I met her, she was not. Apparently her son has a drug problem, has been shot. That sound like fun?

He told me he found me attractive, even when he was leaving. It made no sense. He sent me an e-mail about a year after we separated, telling me he was thinking of me. That also made no sense. WE WERE GETTING DIVORCED!

It has been five years. He signed the divorce papers over Christmas holidays. He says he does not want to co-parent with me (like I have the plague or something). He said he would always be my friend, even if he fell out of love with me. Well, he said a lot of things.

Every time I have a bad day, I think, *This is why he left*. Every time I have a good day, I think, *How could he have left, because I'm awesome?* I wonder if I will ever get over the hurt and the betrayal. I wonder why I wasn't enough.

Things are getting better. I don't cry every day. I don't need to drink a bottle of wine every night to stop the story in my head. In fact, the story, although continuous, is not as loud as it was a few years ago. I know I probably sound like a bitter woman. I don't think this is bitterness. I'm confused. I'm sad. I'm mad. I'm scared. I'm a lot of things. I'm grieving.

I just want to understand. I have a great kid. I have a great family and a great group of friends. But I wonder, *What did I miss?* And I wonder if this is it. Why didn't I see him as this man? I know for a fact there is no way I could ever love this man. This man is horrible. Why did I miss seeing him as this man? What kind of man walks out on his only child, ten years into that child's life?

I think he'd had an emotional breakdown. I think he must be crazy. I think he is probably an alcoholic. I think he is probably a very insecure man deep inside. I think he is a very selfish man on the surface. But then I think, *Maybe it's me.*

But I am working on that . . .

31

The Need to Help

Racquelle from British Columbia, Canada
61 years old
Separated nine years

Who would have thought or guessed that after

- thirty-five years of marriage and friendship;
- eight pregnancies;
- six amazing children;
- adding three great partners that married three of the children;
- twelve loving and wonderful grandchildren;
- twenty-five-plus years of homeschooling;
- being a leader in the church, community, and provincially; and
- owning a family business in the community

the LOVER of my LIFE and FATHER to the amazing six children could just . . . have a bailiff bring over divorce papers on a Sunday afternoon and call it QUITS, say to me on the night before Father's Day that he didn't love me anymore and hadn't loved me for years, and that he had LIVED a LIE that I was unaware of, had no problems "using me" physically (terminology he used), lived a life of no accountability with no interest in being with his own wife and children.

Questions were MANY accompanied by daily sobbing for three years after that day before Father's Day. What was the PURPOSE OF LIFE and LIVING??? Who says an abandoned wife doesn't get PTSD?? I knew I had failed many times over the years, just like any mother and wife does, but why? Why? Why? NO INTEREST in any reconciliation as friends and counsellors continued suggesting and said ours was a reconcilable marriage.

After I DISCOVERED over a period of half a year (he didn't tell me this) that the father to our children was "in love" with one of my good friends—that was a double whammy! She was a family friend who had been to our place for many years for evenings, doing projects together with us for the homeschool organization. She had been a long-distance secretary to my husband, and she was the mother of seven children.

The areas in which I struggled over the years included the following:

- I felt valueless, especially when I had no career to fall back on for income and all I was getting was a minimum-wage job. (I had not had a job for thirty-five years because, among other things, my husband didn't want me to work outside of home because he wanted me to homeschool the children. He would say, "Over my dead body is one of my children going to public school.")
- I experienced loss and loneliness in a world of couples and families.
- I was devastated to the core because my "family life" was gone forever.
- I experienced feelings of being in a pit, HURTING with INNER PAIN and felt as though I couldn't get out.
- I felt helpless and hopeless to continue homeschooling with an absent parent.
- I felt overwhelmed with many areas of life, yet family and friends at that time seemed incompetent and didn't know how to help, and at times they made it worse.
- I dreaded holidays, weekends, and evenings.

A few years after that horrible night, I read about the need to help in the woman's federal prison. I thought it would help me to see women that were in worse situations than mine. So here are all the things I started to do to get my mind off of what I was going through and keep my evenings and weekends as busy as possible.

- Helped in a woman's prison every week
- Became a part of Citizens on Patrol
- Did tutoring
- Taught piano lessons

- Went to sleep every night, listening to June Hunt or music or the Book of Psalms all night
- Helped at the local and surrounding area court house
- Visited widows and singles
- Played piano with a band
- Took dancing lessons
- Drove a motorcycle
- Joined a band and made a CD
- Traveled

Not at all feeling valued by my low-paying jobs, I decided to go back to school for further training. I was accepted to three schools (different careers), and during that time my very good friend (my mother) passed away after a short struggle with cancer. I went off to school a few weeks after her funeral to become a nurse, graduated, and started working for three companies—anything from night shifts to evening shifts to weekends to holidays.

Working was my life that helped with income and kept me distracted. I do realize that abandoned wives and families go through the same sort of grieving process that people who are grieving a death go through, except rejection is a huge part of it. There is no encouragement or support for grieving your loss when "divorced" is stamped on your forehead. It's the opposite—we are shunned.

Support is needed most of the time—not just once a week. It's like hourly and daily. Who has time to give such support? In fact, there is way more rejection than you care to talk about from those around you who are supposed to be close to you. Who can you trust now anyways? So a whole new network of contacts (not necessarily friends) is what has to happen in order for you to function daily. It is definitely a "network" of people, because ONE person could never be there for the deeeeeeep loss that just hit you. I do believe God sees my tears.

As of today, I have hope many more days. I love to help women in helpless situations. There are still questions, and because of the large family I have, there are still many unwanted and undesirable situations and events that are part of the new way of life. I still go one day at a time. After nine years, I can laugh and smile more. My hope for my future is a heavenly perspective—my treasures are laid up somewhere beyond the blue.

32

We Can Do It!

JoAnne from Flemington, New Jersey, USA
62 years old
Separated five years

I was married for thirty-five years. I thought it was wonderful. Unfortunately, my ex must have thought otherwise. He started an affair with his first cousin's wife. I found out that he was having an affair just a few weeks before our thirty-fifth wedding anniversary. My daughter found a message on Facebook that stated, "You are my best friend and lover." This statement will be indelible in my mind forever. I was shocked, devastated, and numb. He walked out the door on December 30, 2010, so that he could celebrate the New Year with her. He came back for two weekends in January only to leave again.

We scheduled marriage counseling in February. He never showed up for the appointment. His paramour worked at a strip mall that had a restaurant. I had a feeling that he was with her, and sure enough, they were in the restaurant having dinner. Needless to say, I walked in and confronted them both. I said to him, "This is what I get after being married to you for thirty-five years? You're here with your whore and your tramp?!?"

He walked me out of the restaurant to my car. I thought we were going to have a conversation. There was no conversation! He turned around and went back to her. I was shocked!!! I walked back into the restaurant and said to her, "You're nothing but a whore and a slut. Your kids hate you. You will have a miserable life and I will see to it." That was the last conversation I had with her.

The next few years were HELL. The divorce took two years and thousands of dollars in attorney fees. His paramour was the driving force in my divorce. She wanted everything, including my china, sterling, and Christmas dolls . . . unbelievable!

My daughter was 13 at the time. Her cousin (my ex's paramour's daughter) was the same age and they went to the same school. My daughter saw her cousin almost every day. This child put my daughter through HELL. She made it a point of letting my daughter know that her new life with my daughter's father was wonderful. In fact, at one point this "child" waited until my daughter was within earshot and made a large announcement. She stated, "My parents are finally getting a divorce, and my 'uncle' can come live with us now." My daughter was devastated. She ran into the restroom in tears.

Her cousin started flaunting her new clothes, designer purses, etc., basically her whole new image. My ex had more money than her father. After the divorce, which was finalized in June 2012, my daughter's cousin and her mother moved in with my ex, thereby making our lives worse. My daughter's relationship with her father was almost non-existent. She had a horrible high school experience. Most days she went to school on two hours of sleep. Her grade point average took a nosedive. She was not accepted to her top-choice college. She decided to go to a two-year college. There, she improved her grades the first year and was accepted to Phi Theta Kappa, an honor society for two-year colleges. After the first year, she applied and was accepted to the college of her choice.

Laughter has been a huge part of our lives. You have to find humor where ever you can. I caught an episode of *The Ellen Show* where she featured a doll called Homewrecker Barbie and told my daughter that I wanted to buy it and send it to his paramour. Her name is Gloria; my daughter coined the name "Whoria." I told her that since Whoria is such a narcissist, I wanted to send the doll, wrapped in beautiful paper, to her place of employment. When she opened it in front of her co-workers, it would be Homewrecker Barbie.

I couldn't find this doll to purchase, so I wrote to the Ellen Online Shop. Ellen got my letter and apparently she too found it funny. She read my letter on air and sent me the doll and the DVD of when she read my letter. No, his paramour never got the doll, but my letter was read on air and was televised everywhere Ellen is. And YES! My ex and his paramour saw this episode. MISSION ACCOMPLISHED! We still tell this story and laugh.

The past five years have been the biggest roller coaster of my life. My daughter and I have had our ups and downs. Most days I felt like I was hovering over my body and that this was happening to someone else—it couldn't be me! There were days I felt like I was on a magic carpet, but I had no steering wheel. My life was out of control.

I did a lot of reading, which helped tremendously. It helped to know that I was not alone. I read *Runaway Husbands, The Gift of Betrayal*, and *Things Happen for a Reason*, to name a few. My mantra was Gloria Gaynor's song "I Will Survive." Our other motto was "Success will be our revenge." I went out and bought a life-size poster of Rosie the Riveter, nicely framed, and put it in a prominent place. I saw this when I got up in the morning and before I went to bed in the evening. The poster says, "WE CAN DO IT!" and we have.

I have learned to change door locks and operate the lawn tractor, which I did not even know how to start prior to my ex walking out the door. We painted the living room and bought beautiful new carpeting and furniture from EBay to replace what he took. I had to rent a very large truck to pick up the furniture from two hours away. My daughter thought I needed a truck license to drive it. I never drove anything that large! It did not even have a rearview mirror, only large side-view mirrors.

I remember telling my daughter the truck was a lot like life. You can't look in the rearview mirror; it's full steam ahead! The room looked better than it did when it had the furniture that he took. I also purchased the marital home. This was a HUGE success. This gave my daughter the stability that she needed, and it helped give me the confidence and knowledge, that yes . . . WE CAN DO IT . . . and we did!

33

Fake It Till You Make It!

Heather from Long Island, New York, USA
32 years old
Separated three years

"Do you want to know why I've been in such a bad mood lately?" he asked me casually as I cleaned up the bedroom, getting ready to put our house on the market. He was lying in bed, having just woken up around ten in the morning, after I had dropped our toddler off at his day care that morning. "Sure," I answered hesitantly, thinking for sure he was going to say, "I cheated on you" or "I found out I have [Insert some horrible illness here]." But instead the words that came out of his mouth were so far beyond my wildest dreams, I just stared at him blankly. "I . . . I'm not sure we are going to work."

Seven years of marriage, ten years together, and 30-year-old me literally could not understand the words that were coming out of his mouth—and not to toot my own horn but I consider myself a bright woman. It has been almost three years since that day in December, but I remember it like it was yesterday. I keep it buried in my secret file cabinet in my brain in case I ever feel like things couldn't get worse, or that I'm not strong enough to handle something that comes my way. I bring it back up at those times and think, "Heck . . . that's right! I handled that like a champ. What I'm going through now is nothing."

I'm assuming, if you are reading this, something similar happened to you. And if I had to guess, you're thinking one of two things: (a) "He'll come back. How could he not?" or (b) "I'm never going to survive the heartbreak I am feeling right now." I can assure you of these two things: (a) you don't want him to come back; you deserve better (One day you will read that and agree. I promise.) and (b) you're not only going to survive; you will be a better, stronger woman because of what you are about to go through. Thirty-year-old me, who thought I was as happy as happy could be, now seems like the shell of the strong, confident, sarcastic, woman I am now because of the battle I went through.

The first thing I did after he told me he didn't think "we were going to work" was have what you could call a slighttttt mental breakdown. There was throwing of the *Friends* disc collection that I was holding in my hand, there was a panic attack rolled up in a ball on the floor, and there was some curling up under the covers and pretending it didn't happen. But then at a quarter to five in the afternoon, I had no choice but to put on my big girl pants, drive to my son's daycare, and pick him up with a smile on my face as if nothing happened.

This was not the last time I would put on a brave face for my son's sake, but if it wasn't for this brave face that I was faking for so long, I wouldn't have realized, "Screw it—it's not a face. I AM brave!" I got home, dropped my son off, and said, "I need to go see my best friend." Now that probably sounds like a normal thing for most people to do, but looking back on it over time I realized that in my seven years of marriage, my ex and I had placed a little bubble around our world and the only people who really knew about our lives were myself and himself. To talk about our problems with anyone else would be to admit that we had problems, so we did what I've come to learn many couples do while in crisis—buy stuff to make us happy and move on with our "happiness!"

So when I called my friend out of the blue and said, "I'm coming over— we need to talk," she knew something was up. I made it most of the drive without crying, not counting when I drove past the hospital where our son had been born. I walked in her door and told her what had just happened to me, and her response was one that I took on for longer than I like to admit. That response was, "Well he can't just leave! That's not how this works. Two of you agreed to be bound for life, and now one of you can't just decide that he doesn't want that anymore." Made sense to me in the moment, but as I type that I can't help but laugh. Of course he could leave if he wanted! We were married, not cell mates in jail.

Two days after he told me, he was out of the house and on his way to North Carolina, and as everything sunk into my head, I came to terms with the fact that I was in desperate need of some counseling to deal with what was about to happen to my life. I called my ex and said, "Here is what we're going to do. You get counseling on your own, I'll get counseling on my own, and then we can meet back up and get counseling together."

I held up my end of the bargain, and through that work my smile became a little bit less fake by the day. I'd forgotten that there was a person living inside of me who wasn't a teacher by day and wife/mother by night. There was a fun-loving, imaginative woman DYING to get out, but I had kept her buried for way too long. Through counseling, I was able to talk about my marriage and my past, and what I needed to do in order to wake up every day and survive what I was going through. On the hard weeks I went twice a week, and used up boxes of tissues in the poor woman's office. On the easier weeks I went once a week and only used half a box of tissues.

Other than going to counseling, I woke up every day, went to work with the fakest smile I could plaster on my face, and taught my students to the best of my ability. My work was my outlet. Besides my best friend, the second person I told what happened was my best friend at work. I thought it was important for someone I worked with to know so that if I was in my office with my door shut, sobbing and listening to Adele, it all made sense. I avoided telling anyone besides those two until I was ready to handle the response that I would get from people. My counselor helped me come up with the words to express my situation that I could say without blubbering through. And once I felt confident in telling my story, I began sharing it with others. I thought it would feel terrifying. But the more people I shared my story with, the more confidence I felt in the fact that I was not just making it through but beginning to carve out my new life.

Almost three years later and I am sitting on my couch, in my townhouse that I share with my loving and amazing almost 6-year-old son who will be starting kindergarten in less than a month. I will be at his first day of school, on my own, waving him goodbye and wishing him luck, and at this point in my life I can say I wouldn't have it any other way. I love the person I am today, and one day I may find someone who also loves the person I am today. I am happy to say that I know for a fact that if I can't find a person who loves me just the way I am today, tomorrow, and for all the rest of my days, I will be just fine on my own. I will keep on keeping on by creating my own happiness and wearing the no-longer fake smile but a true, confident smile that I wear with pride because I put it there all on my own.

34

He Stopped Loving Me
but Forgot to Tell Me

Olivia from California, USA
54 years old
Separated sixteen months

Hi, I'm Olivia from California, and on February 25, 2015, at 7:04 p.m., my husband of twenty-seven years (I'll call him Ned) looked at me and said, "I can't do this anymore" and walked out the door.

That's not entirely true. I need to back up to Sunday, October 5, 2014. That's the date that my world was turned upside down. The day before, I would have said my marriage of twenty-seven years was an eight or nine out of ten. I thought he worshipped me, and many of our friends envied our relationship. We did everything together, but on that Sunday morning he decided not to join me when I went to visit friends—and I have to admit I was hurt, but it wasn't the end of the world.

When I returned, we had a fight about this (probably the first real fight we'd had in years), and I ended it by leaving him behind to go golfing, as we had a tee time already booked. I assumed that he'd pout for five or ten minutes and then join me on the first tee. But he didn't. And he didn't join me on the second nor on the third. Finally, after playing nine holes, I decided that I'd call it a game and go home to talk to him. Never did I imagine that he wouldn't be there. He had left and gone to a hotel. He actually threw his wedding ring out the window as he was driving to the hotel. I was completely blindsided. I had no idea he wasn't happy.

After I had frantically texted him for hours, he finally responded and told me where he was. I was beside myself. To me, it was a normal fight—but to him, he was done.

I met him in the hotel and we talked for an hour, and he agreed to come back home. I still didn't understand what was happening (and I'm not even sure that I noticed his ring was gone). We went to bed together, and the next morning I went to work as usual, after kissing him goodbye and thinking things were OK. When I got home that afternoon, he had his bag and laptop packed and said he was leaving me—and this time he was not coming back.

He left the house to stay with a friend, and I sat on the stairs and cried and cried until I couldn't stand. After three days of not hearing from him (and trying to function normally because I had no idea what was happening), he agreed that he'd meet to talk. I actually told our son that he was away on a business trip. We met and he confessed that he wasn't happy, but he was willing to try to make it work if I was willing to make some concessions from his list. Although the concessions were very one-sided, I was prepared to do anything to make my marriage work.

He returned. We settled back into a routine, and our marriage got ever better (or so I thought). He met me at the door one night with a bottle of champagne and a dozen roses when I came home from work. He had spent the day printing out every picture of the two of us together and spread them across the floor. He said he was so sorry for hurting me and wanted to make things right. For Christmas, he bought a new wedding band and gave me the most gorgeous ring I had ever seen. We went to Florida for New Year's and things were fun and exciting and normal. Then, in February, we went to Jamaica for two weeks with friends, and again the holiday was amazing. There were no signs for me to miss.

We returned on February 25, 2015, and let me go back to my opening sentence—at 7:04 p.m. on the night we returned from a two-week holiday, my husband of twenty-seven years looked at me and said, "I can't do this anymore" and walked out the door. This time I knew he wasn't coming back. I felt betrayed and angry and used. Our sex life in Florida and Jamaica was amazing. For someone who was planning to leave, he didn't show any signs as he slept with me night after night after night. The whole time, I believed that the man who worshipped me was back.

I went to work the next day, and for the next two weeks I didn't tell anyone that my husband was living in a hotel. Our 24-year-old son was living with us at the time, and after a couple of days of his asking where Dad was, I finally broke down and told him. Ned told our second son in the car the following afternoon and sent a text that said, "He understands and all is good." Unfortunately, all was not good, and as soon as his father dropped him off, my son was on the phone looking for answers from me. I went and picked him up but had no answers because I didn't understand anything.

I wasn't in a space to tell anyone, so I left that to him. His texts were all the same: "There's no easy way to say this, but I left Olivia. She'll need your support now and when I get time, I'll talk to each of you." Interestingly, it's now sixteen months later and he still hasn't explained to anyone. And then the questions started from family and friends: "Why?" and "Why didn't you tell us you were having problems?" and "Why did you always act like you were so happy?" I think that was the toughest—trying to explain to friends something I didn't understand at all. Even though I was surrounded by friends, I was so alone. I didn't sleep. I didn't eat. Within a few months, I had lost thirty-five pounds.

We never fought when we were married, and even when we were separated we didn't fight. We started mediation. If I got angry during the mediation, he shut down or walked out. I was desperate for any information about why or what was happening but wasn't permitted to express myself so we did the entire separation agreement without me saying all the things I desperately needed to say. The separation agreement is now signed.

Although he swore there wasn't someone else and he was going to die a lonely man, he is now spending a lot of time with someone else. When she appeared on the scene, I'll never know and really don't think it actually matters. I read books and I've attended therapy (which is crucial), and I still have no answers as to why. I've partially stopped blaming myself. My therapist told me over and over again, "You can't fix what you don't know."

Things are better. I'm back into a routine, and although I do things now and put on a brave face, I'm still really sad and find that I still cry a lot. The days are brighter and clearer, but I'm so angry and feel empty and sad that I often feel as though things would have been a lot easier if he had died rather than just walked out on me.

35

Awakening to a New Reality

Judithe from Tampa, Florida, USA
62 years old
Separated four years

My awakening began late one evening in September 2011 during dinner, when my husband of twenty-five years suddenly announced that he didn't feel connected to me, had mourned the relationship, and moved on. I had been concerned all summer by his strange behavior towards me and our two adult sons, but I thought perhaps it was a phase that some 63-year-old men experience due to aging, erectile dysfunction, depression, health concerns, financial difficulties, marital boredom, or life disappointments.

I was even more surprised when he added that he had already moved out while I was at work and then stubbornly refused to tell me where he had moved other than that he was living with an unnamed "friend." This was most bewildering, since he had always relied on me for the majority of our financial support and decision making. With so much left unsettled, he simply walked out of the door of our home and into the night.

The very next evening, there was an electrical fire in our home—and in less than twenty-four hours, I was husbandless and homeless. That night I moved in temporarily with my elderly, widowed father and filed for divorce. I certainly didn't suspect my husband of having an affair but instead thought that he might have a brain tumor as the explanation for his sudden, irrational behavior. I couldn't sleep and quickly dropped at least fifteen pounds on the "Divorce Diet."

I felt a great deal of anger and betrayal when I discovered that my husband's "friend" was a woman we both knew in recovery and how quickly they were accepted in our recovery community as a romantic couple. Within the safe haven offered by my father, I began an intensive search for friends and professionals to help me navigate this unexpected turn of events. With the help of my dear father, an experienced divorce attorney, some DivorceCare classes, Al-Anon, sponsors, mental health professionals, a financial adviser, the few friends who remained loyal to me, and a weekly meditation class, I began examining myself and my marriage more closely.

In the meantime, my spouse countersued me for alimony and dissipation of assets, which not only added insult to injury but also made the divorce process longer and more expensive. At our mediation, I took responsibility for all marital debt and ultimately filed a chapter 13 bankruptcy proceeding to pay the debt within five years. The bankruptcy was successfully completed in three years.

Up until the moment my husband left that night, I believed we had mutually encouraged and supported each other through the ups and downs of nearly twenty-seven years together as best friends and partners in our marriage, parenting, our careers, and especially in our recovery. We rarely fought or had open disagreements between us, so it was quite horrifying to realize that my husband had been secretly planning to escape our marriage without expressing his unhappiness to me or suggesting ways we might salvage our marriage.

Of course, I continued to scour the Internet and read many books, looking for any intelligent explanation as to how his unhappiness and decision to abandon the marriage with such finality could have happened without raising my suspicions and why I didn't have an equal voice at the end of my marriage. I had read studies about "gray" divorce, but that described a more mutual, amicable decision to divorce between older adults. It wasn't until I discovered the website Runaway Husbands that I finally had a name to describe my traumatic experience and for the first time encountered a supportive community of abandoned spouses in various stages of healing from Wife Abandonment Syndrome.

After reading Vikki Stark's book *Runaway Husbands* and fully comprehending what had happened and what to expect, I could honestly begin the internal healing process and let go of my anger and resentment. I learned that I deserved much better than being discarded in such a cruel and humiliating fashion. I found relief by doing yoga and taking long, solitary walks and, for the very first time, engaged in self-care in the form of massages, manicures, acupuncture, and other healing arts.

The meditation classes provided refuge from the emotional storm of the divorce proceedings and became a very crucial element to regaining my inner calm and peace of mind. I began studying and practicing meditation regularly and in 2013 was invited to travel to Portugal with some of my class members for a festival. This was a turning point for me because I didn't have a passport and hadn't been outside the United States in over twenty-five years. Despite my fears, I obtained the passport and the week in Portugal with my class was absolutely wonderful.

Since then, I have traveled to southern Europe and the Mediterranean, Asia, the United Kingdom, and just recently to Las Vegas and Sedona. Just for fun, I also enjoyed a hot-air balloon ride for my 60th birthday. When my sons graduated from their universities, I drove from Florida to New Jersey and Pennsylvania to attend their graduations as the only parent in attendance. Their father and his new wife didn't attend his sons' graduations and didn't invite them to their wedding just three months after our divorce. My sons now enjoy a good relationship with their father, especially since his divorce from the affair wife after three and a half years of wedded bliss. My sons have also been very supportive of my new life as a single mother.

In the past four years, I have learned that I can depend on a small but loyal group of friends with whom I can share so many wonderful experiences and that I will never again tolerate disrespect or anyone setting limits for me. I continue to meditate daily, attend classes, and also teach meditation. I retired from full-time employment at the end of 2015 and fully enjoy my new life. I exercise regularly and pay close attention to my spiritual, emotional, and physical health and try to assist other women to gain a sense of self-respect and the confidence to create a more fulfilling life through my community's volunteer activities. I love redecorating and renovating my own little house to suit my tastes and traveling to new places. I learned to create and nourish my new identity as an older but wiser single woman entering the last third of life, full of joy and undiscovered possibilities.

36

Operation Truth Bomb

Susan from Orlando, Florida, USA
47 years old
Separated nineteen months

Ta tum, ta tum . . . My husband was talking, but all I could hear was my heart pounding in my ears. It was deafening. Heart racing, mind racing . . . what did he say? He's leaving . . . Why??? Something about not loving me anymore and needing to be on his own. His therapist told him to follow his heart and to do what makes him happy, so he's moving out.

Thinking back, the signs were there. I just didn't see them. Maybe I didn't want to see them. He has been difficult for years, not really enjoying family life. His mom died after a bout with cancer in 2011, and his dad died a few years later. I attributed his distance with me and the kids to those two devastating, life-altering events.

I met Freddy in high school. We dated seven years, and after college we were married. We were the perfect match! We have two amazing kids, and we built a blessed life in a beautiful neighborhood. We rarely argued or even disagreed on anything, which I've come to realize was a symptom of his compliant, non-confrontational personality.

With the precision of a military offensive, he rolled out Operation Truth Bomb in four phases.

Phase 1

The unraveling began on July 3, 2014, when twenty-eight years into our relationship he tells me he that he is dealing with some trauma from childhood and needs "space." He made a point of saying more than once, "I am not happy in our relationship." I immediately shift into overdrive, setting up counseling appointments, offering to do whatever it takes to help him during this difficult time.

I was in counseling within a week of his admission, but it took me several months to get him to go with me. He mumbled through the counseling session with a chorus of "I don't know'" and "maybe." Needless to say, that was his first and last attempt at joint counseling. So I walk on eggshells in our house for several months, giving him space to work things out, although I fear he's pushing me out.

Phase 2

On November 10, 2014, I noticed a charge for an apartment complex on my bank statement. That's odd. I was home that day and he was at work, so I called and left him a voicemail asking him to call me when he had a moment to talk about this charge from Avalon Reserve. He called me back almost immediately to tell me he'd get a sub for his class and come home to talk about that. WHAT? He came home to tell me that he had rented the apartment so that he could move out to gain even more space for his healing.

I beg, I cry, I plead. . . . "How can you make this decision without even discussing it with me? We haven't gotten past the 'I need space' phase. You need to tell me what you are feeling so that we can work through it." It goes on and on for hours. He hardly said a word that day. When he did, he said, "Wow, your comments give me pause." That's it? Wow! I should have pulled the plug right then, but I didn't. He agreed to think about it for a week before moving out. At the end of the week, he tells me he's going to stay and he'll consider cancelling the apartment lease. REALLY? Consider? Why was I still hanging in there? We go on like that for about a week and then, Phase 3 begins.

Phase 3

The inevitable "other woman." I have learned through this experience that "I need space" translates into "I need space to have sex with other women." I'm learning to speak "man-speak." In fact, I'm quite fluent!

On November 17, 2014, he takes me out so that we can talk. He tells me he doesn't know what to do, but he won't move out just yet. He admits that he's having an affair with a friend of ours from high school with whom he had reconnected online. Ta tum, ta tum . . . there it is again. I can't hear what he's saying, only my own heartbeat pounding in my head. What did he say? That's he's sleeping with Cindy? For how long? Did he say a year? And then something about some one-night stands with other women before that? I don't remember much about that night after that. I do remember pulling it together long enough to say that his cheating does not change the fact that I want to do everything in my power to repair our marriage.

I beg him to go back to counseling with me—to no avail. He tells me he needs to think about whether he wants me or Cindy and he'll get back to me. Why am I still in this again?? He gets back to me in a week to tell me that he chooses me, our marriage, our family. GREAT, I think! (Yes, I am still all in! I have no idea why.) So I tell him he must break up with his girlfriend. Yes, that feels as weird to say as it does to read—telling your spouse to break up with his girlfriend. How ridiculous is that? So he does, but it's short-lived. He rolls out Phase 4.

Phase 4

On December 4, 2014, he announces to me that he went to his counselor (so glad he's in counseling!) and she told him that he needs to be true to himself. So, he's moving out and leaving me. He does not love me and he believes that once that's gone there is nothing in the world that can bring that feeling back. He moves out the next night—it was a Friday night. He doesn't take anything with him—no clothes, no furniture. . . . It's like he's running away from something. He didn't even tell our children he was leaving. I made him come back on Sunday and tell them that he was leaving and why and pack up all his stuff for donation. (He told me he didn't want ANY of it.)

I cannot describe the devastation that followed. After he left here (me and the kids in a crying lump on the couch), he went to tell his niece who is like a sister to him that he was moving out and why. She

called it his World Tour of Heartbreak and Destruction. That day was
December 7, 2014, my own personal D-Day.

I lived in the shock phase of recovery for a few months. Joining three
divorce support groups helped me move forward. I'm now eighteen
months beyond D-Day and I'm still in recovery. This experience has
changed me and will forever be a part of who I am. I don't know that
I'll ever label myself as "healed," but I know that I will keep moving
forward thanks to the strength I found in those groups.

I have learned many things from this experience: emotional
heartbreak causes actual physical pain and it's not confined to the
chest—your entire body aches. Midlife crises are real and they are
no joke. Self-centered people make horrible partners. You never
REALLY know someone. And most importantly—I'm so much
stronger than I thought!!!

💔

37

My Dance-Away Husband

Patricia from Peachtree City, Georgia, USA
64 years old
Separated three years

I thought that my husband and I had the most wonderful marriage. Even our friends commented on how well we got along and how much we seemed to enjoy each other's company.

We got married right out of college, after meeting each other our freshman year, and would have been married thirty-nine years in August. But in July everything changed.

Our 8-year-old grandson, who lives in Virginia, came to visit us for the week of July 4th. My husband told me that he had to be out of town on business the weekend we were to take him home, so I would have to drive him back myself—something I had never done before. I successfully drove my grandson from Georgia to Virginia, turned him over to his other grandfather, and spent the weekend with a girlfriend.

On Sunday I headed home. After an exhausting eight-hour drive, I arrived home to find both of my husband's cars gone. When I went into the garage, I noticed right away that all his tool chests were gone, along with his table saw and other items. I immediately picked up my phone and called him to see what was going on. I got an automated message stating that he had blocked my number. I was shocked.

I was literally shaking from head to toe when I went into the house and found a five-page typed letter on the kitchen table, telling me how he needed a different life-style. How all the things he had once loved to do were now just boring and a waste of time. He wanted a life with drinking and dancing every weekend. He said our friends were old and half-dead and bored him. He left the way he did because he was afraid that if he told me face- to-face, he would not have been able to leave. And he couldn't bear to see the look on my face as I watched him move out. I was to contact him only by e-mail going forward. I was to send any mail for him to an address of a friend, which he gave me.

When I had finished reading the letter, I sat at the table shaking and literally screamed at the top of my lungs for almost fifteen minutes. I then called a good friend, who came over to support and comfort me. She took me to her house for dinner because she didn't think I should be alone.

The trauma I went through that day changed me. I remember going grocery shopping the following Monday and seeing all the things going on around me that had not changed. I kept thinking, *How can everything around me be the same when I am so different?* For months afterward, I had trouble concentrating; I couldn't make decisions, I had trouble remembering to eat, and the least little thing brought me to tears. One of the tricks I used to help get me through those early days, when I couldn't understand how such a wonderful husband could have done something so cruel, was to think that aliens had invaded his body. The man I married would never have behaved like that.

More than a year after he left and after our divorce was final, I found out that he had married our ballroom dance instructor. Suddenly it all made sense. Everything he had said in his desertion letter, everything he had said in the one counseling session he came to with me was a lie. I later found out that he married her exactly six days after our divorce was final. I had reluctantly agreed to hire her for dance lessons because I thought it would be a good way for us to reconnect and spend time with each other. I see now that there were many red flags in the year and a half we were taking lessons that I should have seen, but I trusted my husband completely (something I will never do again).

Over time and with a lot of help from very supportive friends, sessions with a counselor, and divorce care classes as well as spending
time with people, I was able to move on with my life. I came to believe
that there were events that occurred about six months before he left
that set his plans in motion. He had a health scare that I think made
him re-evaluate his life. I think he was very depressed and unhappy
with what he had accomplished in his life. He felt like his success in
life was determined by what he did, what his title was at work, how
much money he made, and what he had achieved in his life. He didn't
realize that success is about who you are, not about what you do. It is
based on your relationships with others, your family and friends, and
the impact you have on other people.

In those six months, I had been asking him repeatedly what was
wrong, because I had noticed that he seemed unusually unhappy and
depressed. He would only say that he was just really tired or that he
was having problems at work. I think his state of mind made him a
perfect target for a woman who saw the wonderful relationship we
had together while she was in our home giving us dance lessons, and
decided she wanted that for herself.

It has been almost three years since he left, and I am still amazed at
all the things I have accomplished by myself. I sold our house with
literally no help from him. I bought my own house and did many of
the repairs and improvements by myself. I have driven to Virginia and
back numerous times by myself. I have even driven my grandson down
to Georgia to spend a week with me.

I have been amazed at all the help people have offered me along the
way, many of them total strangers. The book *Runaway Husbands* was
extremely helpful in the early days after he left. It confirmed that it
wasn't my fault and that many other women had experienced the
same emotions and asked the same questions. The other things I have
found to be the most helpful were physical exercise, staying busy,
spending time with people, and helping others. I began walking my
neighbor's dog daily. I volunteer at my church and go out of my way
to help others whenever I can. I find myself more compassionate and
empathetic than I was before this happened to me.

I keep thinking about all the things that my ex is now missing because of his behavior. By his own choice, he has no contact with his son or grandson, and most of his friends have lost all respect for him. Sometimes something will happen that will trigger a memory of how close and happy we once were and how much fun we had together. He chose to dance away from that life and give it all up. I am learning to cherish those memories instead of trying to avoid them as I move on with my life.

38

Family, Friends, and Validation

Maria from Toronto, Ontario, Canada
59 years old
Separated ten years

Before my ex-husband announced to me, out of the blue, that he was leaving our marriage and, yes, our family as it stood, he had been the epitome of a good husband and family man. Even friends had always admired our family unit. Well, on that fateful day, what struck me most was how he had seemed to morph overnight from a caring and loving man to a cruel and devious one. I never saw it coming, nor did either of my two children. This terrible event forever changed the course of our lives but did not, thankfully, deter our triumphant recovery.

I could not understand (and still don't) how someone who supposedly loved you could be so heartless and smug about his marriage and family. You see, he also announced at the same time that he had someone new—a woman from his past. This horrible day happened many years ago, in December 2006, just before Christmas and an already-planned family vacation to an island!! Timing is everything, no???

For two weeks, I tried to reason with him, understand what was going on, and convince him that our family was worth saving! I begged him to work out whatever was going on with him or with us. I would have done anything to save the marriage and our family. I would have even forgiven him for cheating. I should mention that during those two weeks, I told no one about what was going on (including the children). Even though I found out months later that he had already told numerous people, I was hoping, at the time, that things could be worked out with the man I loved and that my children could be spared from this sad state of affairs, no pun intended!

Both of my children believed our family was special, and they were proud of it. My daughter had even written about the love of her family at school, leading teachers to let us know how special it was for them to read her stories. I was very angry with him for never considering the children. So, at the end of the two weeks, I realized it was impossible to save the family because he had already made up his selfish mind. He was wearing blinders and was not interested in doing a single thing to preserve our family. My children and I had been blindsided, and he was as cold as ice. He was now more interested in his new life.

When my children were told, they were devastated. Undoubtedly, they were in shock. I will never forget what they said to him. My daughter told him that he should try to save the marriage and family. You see, he had always told the children to try and never give up. My son said he would give up baseball if he tried to make things work. Of course, my ex-husband did not hear a thing. I am sure he was too busy thinking about flying out that same night to see his girlfriend in another country. Well, that was before he realized that I had hidden his passport!!! No one was going to leave my children after delivering such a horrible blow to them.

Right there and then, I decided to surround my children and myself with people who loved us and who had our backs. I forgot about the people who sided with my ex (some, I am sure, with self-serving motives), those who forgot about us, those who listened to his "rewritten" history of our life together, and those who said there are always two sides to a story. To this day, I still know in my heart that what he did was wrong and unacceptable. My children and I did not deserve it. My family and good friends validated that for me. This was extremely important in my healing, by the way. From the beginning, I took no responsibility for what proved to be "his" betrayal of our marriage vows and his lack of family loyalty, love, and commitment. Today, thankfully, I still believe in the importance of family, and so do my children!

What also helped my children and me get through this awful time in our history was to continue our lives as we had always done. That included school and homework, religious holidays, birthday parties, sporting commitments/events, trips, time spent together, family functions, and time with friends. We trudged forward with the help of our family and "good" friends, people who are still in our lives today. Of course, along the way, there was still much sadness, disbelief, and anger—but we focused on the good in life and making new memories together.

As well, I took the initiative to get a child therapist for my children and a therapist for myself. There was a mediator during the separation that also helped my children and me. This made the process of healing easier. I talked to a deacon at a church, a psychologist (a cousin of a friend), and all the teachers of my children so they could also help out. One friend found an effective divorce lawyer for me.

I will be eternally grateful to those people who have always stood by us and stood up for us. In the world today, we need more people standing up for those who are wronged. Those affected need validation! I have heard too many stories like mine in this sometimes easily disposable society. Families need to be preserved.

Today, my children are doing very well. My daughter has graduated from university with honours and is working. My son is in his second year at university. Yes, he is still playing baseball! They are happy people and hard workers. I am most proud, though, of their character traits. They are amazing human beings. They are kind, generous, considerate, loyal, and beautiful on the inside and out. We have a lovely bond, and we are there for one another. They understand the importance of family commitment. I know they will carry these traits into their own marriages in the future. They have a relationship with their father (which I believe is important), but they do not want a relationship with his new wife (the woman from his past).

For me, even though I have dated occasionally, I have not met someone special. My children, family, and friends would like nothing more than for me to share my life with someone. Well, initially when everything happened, I needed to recover emotionally and to focus on my children, who have always been a priority. I also had to learn to trust again. I do hope to meet someone with an amazing soul, but for now I live a very active life. I am happy and content with my children, my close family, and my true friends. I continue to surround myself with good people and have had many memorable and beautiful experiences since that fateful day in December 2006.

I would like to conclude by saying that, as my wise lawyer once said to me, we all need validation. I now want to validate what you have been going through as well!

39

Top Tips for Surviving

Fiona from Leicester, England, UK
51 years old
Separated four years

I wanted to write my full story, but I found that trying to do so bought too many raw emotions back to the surface that I don't want to go through again, so I decided to be upbeat and offer some top tips to surviving the Runaway Husband. I hope they help somebody someday, just as the book *Runaway Husbands* did so much to help me realise that I was not the only one this had happened to.

1. Take care of yourself. Sleep, eat, exercise.
2. Learn to love YOU, as you are a beautiful, courageous, woman. Find yourself! You may have been told "this is all your fault," but the words came out of somebody else's mouth and are about them—not you.
3. Cry when you need to. Let it out, even if that is for years. It will stop when it's ready.
4. Don't waste your energy on trying to understand why. You may never know. Put your energy into you.
5. Talk, talk, talk. Get it out to friends and family. Best of all, get a counsellor. It changed my life.
6. Friends who have been through the same thing are a tremendous support. It's a two-way process—you can help them too.
7. Don't hide away too much. You will need quiet time, but don't isolate yourself—connect.
8. Practice gratitude. Be grateful for small things: a hug from your son, a warm day, ten minutes of peace.
9. Acknowledge that life is different now, that's all—not worse,

just different—and you have a great opportunity now to explore and have new experiences.

10. Take small steps. Whatever you need to do next—take it slow and small achievements will get you closer to that bigger goal.

11. Explore your spiritual side—it may need a boost. Find what works for you.

12. This is harsh but—accept that he has left, he doesn't care about you now as he used to. It's so hard to comprehend, but get yourself a good solicitor and get savvy about the money. If you have joint accounts, take your money now before he takes all of it. (I would never have believed mine would have done that to me, but he did.)

13. Treat yourself when you can—massage, book, walk in the park, new nail varnish—you are worth it!

14. Give to others and open your eyes. You are not the only person going through troubled times. This is quite grounding.

15. Be you—because you're bloody amazing!

I hope my tips help. The journey is hard and now as I reflect back, I don't know how I survived it—but I did! I was amazing! Wow, I can't believe I said that. I have become a new person and I am ever evolving. I'm happy, I have amazing friends and family, and I have met loads of new people and a new partner who is brilliant for me and gorgeous. I have my sons around me. They hardly see their Dad, which is not what I wanted for them, but they give me hugs, tell me they love me, and share their life experiences with me. Wow, what a rich life I have.

I also got remarried—to myself! I made vows and bought myself a gorgeous ring. Now I love me, I'll stick by my side and care for me when I'm not well or when I need a hug. How marvellous it is to love oneself.

Take care, ladies. Days will be dark and you may think you can't go on, but take it one day at a time. It will get better and you will have new experiences and adventures that you never would have done when married. Welcome to the second part of your life—enjoy. :)

Namaste

40

Coping! Still Hoping . . .

Barbara from San Antonio, Texas, USA
54 years old
Separated eight months

My marital problems began when my husband accepted an executive position with an NBA team. He felt uncertain about his ability to do it, and he gave his all to the work.

This meant his coming home later and later, never taking a day off, and becoming more and more of a loner—sullen, short-tempered, choosing to watch TV in a separate room rather than be with me. He was not willing to talk about things. Everything I said bothered him. We were not getting along in the days before he ran, but I thought this was nothing a marriage doesn't experience and work through.

One day, my husband texted me the following: "Talked to my mom this a.m. I don't think she's doing well. I'm going to spend a few days over there." Already so offended that he spent so little time with our daughter and me, I texted something snippy back: "Please do what you feel is necessary to maintain this very important relationship. Please define 'a few days' by number and explain what your involvement will be in the lives of your daughter and wife. Thank you very much."

I did not see him again. I found messages on our answering machine from medical clinics and pharmacies indicating that he was sick. One night, my daughter and I went to his mother's house to see how he was and learned he was out of town with the team. I decided to give him time. This is not the first time he had "run away," having gone before for a few hours, a night at most.

Two weeks later, the phone rang. "Hello?" I said, and heard his voice. "I'm done. Our marriage is over," and he hung up.

At different points in our marriage, we have sought counseling. We both believe in counseling, in having an objective intermediary help us to talk through our issues. While I knew he was growing more distant, he never gave an indication that his leaving was a possibility.

Ironically, we have been advocates of marriage, volunteering for twelve years with the Engaged Encounter program as presenters giving the Sacrament talk about how marriage is a covenant, not a contract, and thus a more profound and meaningful faith-based commitment!

And we had recently started in our parish's formation ministry for engaged couples, meeting with them couple-to-couple to share our experiences of marriage and to encourage them to work through any difficulty, explaining there is no reason to end a marriage when one has made such a commitment in faith. This was his portion of the presentation—the "nothing should end a marriage" talk. Even as he left, we were in the middle of working with one of the loveliest couples we had encountered, deeply committed to each other and open to the idea of marriage being forever. I had the uncomfortable task of telling them that my husband had left me and that we could not finish our sessions with them.

He left in October. My phone calls, e-mails, text messages, all go unanswered. He continues to pay the bills, but he now has his own apartment (I don't have the address). He spends money like water (bank statements come to my house), and he recently traded in the car we own jointly and bought himself a new car.

He has no one else in his life except his mother. There is not another woman. He has married his job and thus cannot have a relationship with wife or family. He irrationally blames me as the sole cause of our demise, of his deteriorating relationship with our daughter, of his low self-esteem. He takes no blame for anything.

As I write, we are not divorced. But we are also not reconciled. Throughout these months, I continue to reach out to him in lovingly worded e-mails and texts. Until my daughter graduates from high school next year, I cannot myself file for divorce—working for a Catholic high school, I don't make enough money to support myself and her, so my financial security lies in remaining married to him. He has not, to date, objected to paying our bills and I am not profligate with money.

Not until the six-month mark did I begin to feel the cloud of sadness and tragedy lift. The following things helped me through those first painful months:

1. As a mother, I had to function for my daughter, to show her strength, and to continue to be by her side.
2. As a high school English teacher, I had to put on the persona of a person who is there for her students, giving her all to them, leading them through the plots of novels and dissecting the characters to their core. (I found funny how many men in literature run from the responsibilities of life—in an all-girl school, this makes for fascinating discussions and sharing of their stories!)
3. The faith community of my parish, where I sing in the choir and participate in various ministries—helping others helped me to keep my own sufferings in perspective.
4. Friends, who let me cry, who listened, who advised, who gave me time.
5. Reading books, including Vikki Stark's *Runaway Husbands*, which showed me that this abandonment is more about his inner struggles than my being a bad wife.
6. Finally, prayer . . . I have spent hours reading Scripture, sitting in chapel, meditating, and praying for myself and for him—I pray that my heart may remain open and that I may come "to accept what I cannot change," and I pray for his heart to be softened.

Somewhere inside him that flame of love still flickers. While accepting what is, I continue to live in hope. But I am moving forward . . .

A friend of mine recently lost her husband to abandonment and she is devastated. In my journal, I wrote this: "I wish I could spare her the hours of crying, the self-doubt, the bewilderment over how a man who swore he would be true to her forever could now hurt her like this, the feelings of being a non-person to him and all who worship him, of having to find her identity now that she is without him, of doubting even God's love for her—but I can't. She will have to work through those feelings herself, minute by minute, hour by hour, day by day, week by week, month by month. They are slow, long, and difficult but they do pass. With the help of friends and loved ones who listen and hold our hands, the healing of time comes and we women, brought so low by our men, rise again, stronger and better."

I feel stronger and better. I am beginning to feel happy. I will, however, remain sad that this man whom I love so much will have nothing to do with me. Vikki Stark writes, "A woman doesn't have to be perfect to be a good wife." I cling to this thought. For a time longer, I continue to be a good wife, to be open, to be loving in my communications, to pray for him and us, and to wait.

41

Stunned

Eryn from St. Paul, Minnesota, USA
42 years old
Separated seven months

My husband and I had been together for thirteen years and were celebrating our tenth wedding anniversary. We went to supper, and when I returned from the bathroom I noticed he was texting a woman. I saw the words "love you" and "soon." I felt sick, and the waiter chose that moment to come over with a champagne toast for our anniversary!

I was upset but had to leave with my 8-year-old daughter to help a friend. I thought we would talk about it later, but there wasn't a later. I waited and called him at eleven that evening, midnight, and one in the morning, leaving messages, crying and begging him to call me. I finally got a text at four in the morning saying that he was living with a friend and wasn't coming back. Never in my life did I imagine getting dumped by text on my tenth wedding anniversary.

I have two boys from a previous marriage, and my husband had been parenting them for thirteen years. They are 17 and 15 now. We have a daughter together who is 9. It was so difficult to tell my daughter that her dad was gone, literally disappearing overnight. My boys were furious at him for many reasons, and especially because he had lied to them weeks earlier, saying that we were planning to separate and that it was a mutual decision!

So it has been seven months now and my children and I are still climbing through the wreckage. He is fighting to have fifty-fifty custody of our daughter and is completely ready for his girlfriend to step into the role of new replacement mom, and for her kids to be her fun new siblings. He doesn't care how much everyone is hurting—he just wants everyone to be completely on board with his fabulous new life.

I was in crisis mode the first few weeks before the sadness and anger hit me. I just could not believe he was so willing to just throw us all away like garbage. I read so many books, but what helped me start moving forward was accepting that he was never going to feel bad about what he did to me and my kids. He was a different person than who I thought he was. Once I accepted that my husband and the father of my children was completely gone, I was able to start moving forward. He may as well have been dead, he was so different from the man I knew. I copied parts of the Vikki's book and kept them in my purse to remind me that I could get through it for my kids.

42

My Baby . . . He Wrote Me a Letter

Diane from Hickory, North Carolina, USA
55 years old
Separated four years

It all began as a regular Friday. I only work half day on Fridays, and I use that time to run errands and prepare for the weekend. WE had plans with our best friends for that weekend. I had talked to my husband, Mark, the evening before, as he works out of town during the week.

I arrived home and saw that my daughter was also home. At the time she was 23. I could tell by her face that something was wrong. She told me that Mark had come home, packed a small bag, left a note on my vanity, and left. I thought this strange, but he has always traveled for work since before we were married.

I guess I should start from the beginning. Mark and I met in October of 1979. I was 19 and he was 20. I was working at Footlocker at Tyson's Corner Mall in Vienna, VA. Mark's brother Will also worked at the store. One day when Mark was home from college he stopped by the store to visit his brother, and Will introduced us. I did not have that "love at first sight" moment.

Will and I were good friends and I enjoyed meeting Mark, just as I enjoyed meeting his other family members when they came by the store. But unbeknownst to me, I made quite an impression on Mark. By early December, Mark had visited the store quite often. The Footlocker Christmas party was coming up and Will suggested I ask Mark. I did, and that was the beginning of our relationship.

We had the typical twenty-something relationship. He had transferred to the local university, and we continued to see each other often. Our relationship grew in love and maturity and through the ups and downs of college. He was in school. I continued working full time, though I had moved on from Footlocker.

We became engaged and married on October 23, 1983. Mark had graduated and was starting his career. We bought our first town-house. To save money, we lived in his mom's basement while our home was built. Three years later, I became pregnant with our first child, a son, Brett. Did I mention that he traveled for his job? Because, yes, he missed the birth of our son because he was out of town on business. This became a theme in our marriage.

We then bought our first house, and soon after we welcomed our daughter, Lauren, to the family—the perfect family, in my mind.

Fifteen years later, Mark made a career change and we made the big move to Hickory, North Carolina. This was an adjustment for me, as Mark had his job and the social aspects of that and plenty of travel. I was trying to adjust to being away from my family for the first time and help our children adjust to being "the new kids" in a small south-ern town.

The years progressed. We raised our children, we dealt with the teenage years, we were a family. He went through a few more jobs in the Hickory area and then he landed a job in Mt. Airy, North Carolina, ninety miles from Hickory. He was there Monday to Thursday, and home Friday to Sunday.

Fast-forward fourteen years, and we come to "THE LETTER"

The letter was placed on my vanity in mid-September. The letter began with the dreaded words, "This is the hardest letter for me to write." What! He is writing me a LETTER! Devastation and panic sets in. The words just melded together—I don't even know if I actually read them. But certain phrases stick in my brain:

"I have felt like this for a long time."

"Our marriage has run its course."
"I can't continue to pretend."
"I fell out of love with you some time ago."
"There is no one else."

Our marriage has run its course!!!

And yes, I truly had no idea. I had dealt with taking care of my mother for the past ten years as she slowly slipped away from Alzheimer's. Mark had suffered a cardiac event the previous December 2011 and again in April 2012. Did he change during that time? Yes, but I was told to expect this and just support him. He focused on his health, his fitness, his life. I look back now and see that this was his turning point. Me, I loved and trusted him completely and tried to make our home life as stress free as possible.

So back to the letter, again, A LETTER! He wrote me A LETTER! I try to contact him, but of course he did not answer. Lauren is devastated. She realizes now that her dad is never coming home and he never even said good-bye.

I called my best friend, Lisa. Her husband was Mark's best friend. They had no clue he was thinking of this. His family, his friends, our neighbors, our children were shocked,.

This is where things get messy. He wanted to take one of our dogs. I refused to let him do that. He retaliated and I ended up with a black eye. He did not want me to hire a lawyer. He was going to handle the whole separation and divorce. I hired a lawyer and in his mind, it was game on. For two years, he exhibited only anger and resentment toward me. He did not want me to have anything. We sold the house. I leased my first place on my own, and my new life had begun.

How did I come out of the devastation, the hurt, the disappointment, the fear, the betrayal? I got angry—really, really angry. Or as my mom would say "I got my Irish up." I was not going to have devoted my entire adult life to this person, raise our children basically on my own, and let him just walk away without bearing any responsibility. He disrespected me completely by writing a letter. So I hired a wonderful lawyer. I persevered. I wore him down. He acted like an ass every time we had mediation until I hired the mediator I wanted and took control of the divorce. I got a great settlement, and every day is a new day.

I took an improv workshop and went on stage for the first time doing improv comedy. I auditioned for a musical at our local community theater. I had never sung in public, but I sang a rendition of "You Are My Sunshine" that I had always sung to the kids. And you know what? I got the part. Theater has been my lifeline back into society because, as you know, your friends change after you divorce. The theater is a safe place, a place to safely fail, a place to shine. I think I chose this venue of change because Mark had always said that was something he could never do. And I did it and I am successful.

I deal with the anger every day. Soon after our divorce, Mark married the woman he had been having a long-term affair with while working in Mt. Airy. The kids are continuing their relationship with their dad, but they do not respect him. My kids, friends, and family are proud of the way I have struggled through this devastating time.

I followed the motto Fake it till you make it, and as each day, week, and year passes, I have to fake it less and less. Am I healed? Have I forgiven him? No! I think this type of forgiveness is entirely overrated. He has shown me nothing but anger, resentment, and disrespect since the day he left. Why is he angry? I don't know, but I like to think it is because I took control of my life, my happiness, and my future— something that I am sure he thought I could not do. I think my mom and dad would have been proud. I know my children are.

Every day is a new day.

43

Even the Dog

Trudy from Houston, Texas, USA
62 years old
Separated two years

On a Sunday in the month of July, my husband and I met friends for an early dinner at a casual restaurant. Good food, conversation, laughter, drinking, and catching up. As we left, and our car doors closed, he said rather quietly, "I've taken an apartment."

"What? What are you talking about?"

"I've taken an apartment for a year."

"For a YEAR? What ARE you TALKING about?"

I must not understand what he said. It's summer. . . . He said, "I have spoken to two attorneys. Because we have been married so long, it'll be fifty-fifty." What will be fifty-fifty? He's spoken to attorneys??? OMG, what is happening?

I pleaded, "What are you talking about?" What am I hearing? What is happening?

He said, "I'll get my keys to the apartment on Tuesday. My rented furniture is coming on Wednesday. I'll be gone on Wednesday."

What??? I was feeling my heart sink to my groin. My husband is leaving me? This can't be happening. Not to US. Not to me. What is he saying? This CANNOT be! We've been through so much together. We're devoted to each other. We are a united, loyal family. We're facing old age together. I saved his life when he had a heart attack overseas a year and a half ago. What is going on? How did he come to this outlandish and sudden decision? Where do I fit into this picture? What??? My life is about to change so drastically? So suddenly? Where was I all the time he was deciding this and seeing attorneys, apartments, and furniture? WHAT?????????

The rest of the ride home is a blur. I think I was going into shock. Trauma. I couldn't think straight. The next two days while he was in the house I must have been in denial. The situation was unfathomable. Unthinkable. Ludicrous. There had been no signs. No dialogue. No discussion. No ultimatum.

I asked again what he meant. I wanted him to define his "year in an apartment." I wanted to know what this separation meant. He said "fifty-fifty," but he could NOT mean DIVORCE! He never said the word "divorce" . . . that must have meant he needed some time" . . . that there was hope. Did I forget and deny that he'd mentioned attorneys? Would we see other people? He didn't answer. Could he break his lease? "Yes," he said. On his way out the door, he promised this did not mean divorce. I asked him to be honest. He promised again, "This apartment did not mean divorce." He assured me I could afford to stay in the house for ten years. He planned to be back every Wednesday to pay bills and collect the trash. "I'll just be around the corner," he said.

His answers to my questions encouraged me to be in denial. Even though he handed me a card for a divorce attorney to call, he reinforced his promise that this apartment did not necessarily mean divorce. He assured me that he would be right around the corner in a nearby town. He said he could break his lease. His plan was to come home every Wednesday to take the trash and pay the bills. He would come by to walk the dog. He would still go with me on a planned trip in a few days, but when we got back to the airport after the weekend, he firmly stated that he would go straight to his apartment and I would go to the house. He would NOT be coming home.

Is he serious? Why wasn't I clued in before all this was decided? He told me I would be able to stay in the house for ten years, yet he was also promising his move carried no certainty of divorce. I asked him to be honest, again and again. He mentioned friends of ours who separated and now have a strong marriage.

What? This isn't making sense: It'll be fifty-fifty. I could stay in the house for ten years, but he also promised that our marriage wasn't necessarily over. I cancelled the trip.

Completely holding on to his parting promises, I gave him linens, a can opener, extra dishes, extra silverware, food. He took a lamp from his closet. He must have already gathered other things. He gathered more. I'm in shock. I'm in denial. I've been blindsided. I don't get it.

Why won't he define or acknowledge the separation agreement I'd found online that suggested therapy once a week, dating each other once a week, agreeing not to see other people, and not to change our financial situation yet? He's acting deaf. He will not respond.

I made dinner. I chose denial, thinking he could not be leaving me like this. Impossible. We've been married THIRTY-FIVE YEARS. No recent arguing. No heated issues every day. But I was also devastated. I ask him how we would tell the children. What about our son's engagement party? The invitations have just gone out. Yesterday. The party is in six weeks. About a hundred people are invited to our house.

My husband suggests we not tell the kids until after the engagement party. I say that I can't do that. I can't cover for him. What if our daughter comes by? What if our son calls? No. That isn't right. My husband said, "The kids will get over it. This happens all the time."

Very cavalier. No remorse. I think, "Our kids might learn to live with this, but they will never get over it." This happens to *other* families. Our family is devoted to each other. We have each other's backs. Always have.

I send an e-mail to him, to the next room where he is, an article from the web about the effect this could have on our adult children. He seems totally uninterested. He said he didn't read it. He isn't responding to my asking for a definition of our situation. Why is he so aloof? Why is he calm? Does this mean he isn't serious, and there are other issues going on? No way could he be this heartless. I'm being ABANDONED? It cannot be! No discussion. A done deal. An apartment. But he'll be back every week.

At some point before my husband left very early on Wednesday morning, to the best of my ability to remember, we had the following conversation. I barely responded. I was shocked, STUNNED, unprepared, and bewildered. I was still so "in" the marriage that I was trusting and still valuing his opinion as he spoke. I listened with dismay. What was he saying? I cried. I was shaken by his coldness and hard stare. Only after weeks of ruminating, losing myself, in a traumatic state of not even being able to find the thermostat in the house, paralyzed, not functioning, am I able to have rebuttal thoughts to most of what he said.

Him: "I want this over in four months."

Me: "What? A divorce? In four months? I can't do that."

Him: "You spent too much money on the house. I don't need all this. I hate this house. I hate everything in it. I don't need the gardeners. I don't need any of this. We could have had a second home, which I would have liked. I did everything I could to please you and it was never enough. Didn't we do enough to this house? And you still want new kitchen counters!"

Me: "I have not talked to you about new kitchen counters for YEARS."

It IS enough for me! Where is this coming from? You vetoed the counters a long time ago. Yes, you know how much I love our house. I didn't make it nice out of greed for myself; it was for all of us. I did not spend wildly on furs, jewelry, or insisted on designer clothes or vacations. I bought clothing on sale. I never begged for vacations. Sometimes I color my hair at home to save money! You've seen me do that. I take such good care of our things so they don't need replacing. We've had the same dishes since we got married —the same everything. But I've heard this before . . . that I care too much about the house. Is this the real reason he is leaving? What the fuck?

Him: "I am tired of paying your bills."

MY bills? You mean we are already separate? How does this work? MY bills? I thought it was OUR bills. When did you start thinking this way?

Him: "You put two new bathrooms downstairs. Wasn't one enough?"

I showed the floor plans to you many times. Why didn't you veto what you didn't want?

Him: "You see the cup as half empty. I see it as half full."

I love my house. The cup is full. Projection! It sounds like you see our marriage as half empty.

Him, scoffing: "Cash, plus credit cards? Isn't that enough?"

I never said it wasn't enough, nor did I feel it wasn't enough. I thought it was plenty. Way plenty. Why didn't you tell me if that was out of whack? Why didn't you sit me down and have a conversation?

Him: "You self-actualized. You did the house. You did the garden."

What? I remember studying psychology in college, but I doubt you came up with that phrase. So your therapy became about us? I assumed the therapy you began after your heart attack was about your mortality and retirement. You sound angry and jealous that I have been happy.

Me: "Why didn't you take me to therapy?"

Him: "You weren't interested."

Me: "That's a lie."

Him: "You called me names. No, you didn't call me names."

Are you so mixed up? Can you hear yourself telling lies? Actually, you were the one who called me names. Sometimes the kids were called names. That wasn't my style. I was never that way. I remember you calling all of us "a bunch of jerks."

Him: "I had to buy clothes at Lee Brothers."

What? Their clothes were fine! I couldn't get you into a store to buy clothes for yourself because you hated shopping. You wanted clothes from Land's End because they could be ordered online, they could accommodate your size and height, plus you liked their quality and price for working in the store. You hoarded the better clothes I bought for you, and you hardly ever wore them! They would hang in your closet until the collars went out of style.

Him: "I always drove the old car. I never got the new car."

You were content with the older car because your car was used for the store. Many employees drove your car, and it smelled like sweat. We both drove "my" car when we went out, on a road trip, or you drove it by yourself whenever you wanted to drive it.

Him: "We have different interests. I am interested in nutrition. And exercising. I have a trainer. You won't even walk the dog. I see women at the dog park who are there before they go to WORK. You never even WORKED."

Me: "Are you telling me that you place no value on my being at home?"

Him, flatly, sternly, and looking straight in my eyes: "YES, NO VALUE."

WHAT??? This is my husband? The one who says he is "evolved?" NO VALUE? He is taking away my life's purpose. He is being so cruel. He is slaughtering me. He is destroying me. I reared the children. I took care of everything at home. Everything. I planted almost every tree, bush, and flower in our yard. I never even asked him to stop for milk. . . . WHAT???

Him: "People don't change. You can't apologize for who you are."

So you're telling me I am worthless? No value? You don't like who I am? Suddenly?

Him: "I hate this house. I HATE EVERYTHING IN IT. Everything here is what you chose. It's all yours."

WOW! Out of the blue. What? You've enjoyed our house and have been proud of it. You never seemed interested in furnishings. Where were you? Why didn't you speak up when it was happening if you cared to help choose? You had no interest, and certainly no patience with design or organization. We've been in therapy . . . if this was a problem for you, why didn't you talk about it?

Me: "Why didn't you ever tell me you hated this house? We could have moved and downsized if I knew how strongly you felt."

Him: No answer.

Him: "You kept telling me not to come home early."

Me, beginning to cry: "I must have seen insane! I came to look forward to you coming home early. Remember when Dr. Meyer said our clocks need to synch? I wasn't ready for your retirement. We should have gone to therapy or had some heart-to-heart talks about it. Retirement can be a tough transition for both people. But I took good care of you. And I became used to it and happy about it."

It was too late. He didn't want to hear me. He chuckled at me. He scoffed!! He had so much venomous ANGER.

Him: "You had the kitchen table refinished just after I had the driveway resealed. You couldn't give me break."

That is not the way I remember it. I planned ahead so the table top would be gone during the ten days we would be away. I didn't know your time frame with the driveway! You're spinning this and making me into a monster! It was a lack of communication. I am not a monster. Besides, YOU added an additional vacation a few months ago when we already had two trips planned. This added cost was way more money than refinishing the table top.

Him: "You always said, 'It's my house and I just let you live here.'"

Me: "We all, including you, and the kids, used to joke about that when you put the house in my name in case you were sued at the store. We would all laugh."

Him: "You never embraced my family."

YOU had trouble with your family. You didn't like being around your brother and complained about him and his wife. You thought your sister was cold. You said your mother never had the tools to be a nice person. We were on the same page. You wanted to leave your family gatherings before I did. I always included them. I even included your sister's brother-in-law in everything we did at our house. Didn't I just offer this past week to help your brother-in-law with your sister's unveiling? We were on the same page about my family too!

Him, angrily: "When the kids were little we should have given them chores. After dinner you would ask me to take out the trash! You should have asked our son! You had me CRAWL at their elementary school to get closer to the stage to take pictures. You used me as your WHIPPING BOY! I didn't even want to be there!"

Why couldn't YOU delegate the trash to our son? You make it sound like I wanted you to crawl through World War II trenches in the school auditorium! All of the parents were crouching down as they made their way to the stage to take closer pictures of their young children. That school was the best. You suggested putting the school in our will if something should happen to all four of us! You suddenly didn't like that either?

Him: "Our son wasn't nice to our friends' daughters when we saw them. And we should have stepped in more when our daughter was in high school. They don't respect me."

Is he is going to get rid of the whole package? It kind of sounds like it. Does he resent taking care of the kids? This is getting past crazy. Has he lost his mind? He is unhappy with the kids?

Him: "You were a helicopter mom."

Wait, isn't that the opposite of what you just said? You just said we should have been on top of the kids more.

Me: "I don't think so. I was always the parent who didn't know what test or assignment other parents were worried about. I wanted them to take responsibility for themselves. Yes, I was involved and interested in their lives, but I wasn't a helicopter mom."

He has attacked my homemaking skills, my love and upkeep of the house, my child rearing, my hobbies, my LIFE. My IDENTITY. Can he really believe all the things he's saying? Why has he rewritten everything in such a negative way? What the fuck is happening here?

Him: "I felt left out when our first child was born."

Our first child is 31 years old. Have you gone insane?

Him: "You once called me a clown. No man wants to be called a clown."

Me: "I told you then, I meant jokester."

He scoffed. Loudly. Animated again. He was cold. I still couldn't grasp how strongly he was out to annihilate me.

Him: "You know people will take sides. That's the way these things go."

Me, in such dismay and tears: "Do you love me?" Knowing, just knowing he would say yes. There could be no other answer. He is just very angry and upset.

Him: "I don't hate you. I don't wish you harm."

My heart sunk to my toes. I'm his best friend! OMG. I can't believe it. He doesn't love me? Now he looked at me like he couldn't stand me. I'M BLINDSIDED.

Him, glaring at me: "We haven't had sex in months."

Because your shoulder hurt from surgery, because you were brooding, because you worried about ED. I was being patient.

Him: "I don't desire you anymore."

What did you say?

Me: "I do you." He scoffs and looks at me like I am nothing. Nobody. Dirt. A COLD, HARD STARE. RUTHLESS.

Me, crying: "I don't even believe in divorce."

He scoffs again. He actually LAUGHED. Laughed out loud.

Him: "We will see the kids separately."

Me, crying harder: "This is so fucked up. You are my go-to person when things are bad!"

Him, with a fierce, stone-cold look, said flatly: "Yeah, it is fucked up."

OMG!!!!!!

Him: "I am looking forward to the next phase of my life."

What? You've thought about the NEXT PHASE OF YOUR LIFE? How can this major, horrible thing happen in a matter of hours?

When did he become this person I don't recognize? The next phase of your life? None of these reasons warrant blowing up our lives and our family! We believed in therapy when things weren't going well. I called you a clown? That's a reason?

Me: "Will you see other people?"

Him: "It's not out of the question."

A knife went through my heart. I had read somewhere, "My heart turned to liquid and it began to evaporate." I thought it was a beautifully phrased idea when I read it. Now it has become a description of his heart. My heart was broken. His had evaporated.

Me: "Is this how you left your first wife?"

He doesn't answer. He just looks at me, startled. Because it was.

It was how he left his first wife.

After he left the house, I left him a cell phone message that our friend who just retired as a psychiatrist says that it is very important how we tell the children, even adult children (who, she emphasizes, do not get enough press for the hurt and damage this will cause them). She suggested we tell them as a family, together, even if we use Skype™ for our son in another city. She added that it would not be unreasonable to have our son fly in for a family meeting.

My husband returns my call. His voice is full of anger: "I'll do it [tell the children] MY way! And I will NOT go to therapy with you, and I DO want to see other people." DIALTONE.

OMG. He said seeing other people wasn't out of the question.

About an hour later, my son called me, upset and stunned at his dad's news.

Me: "What is he going to do about your sister?" Son: "He's calling her now."

OMG. My children are shocked and devastated too. And he's telling them on the phone? Out of the blue? And our daughter is local! What a fucking coward! Now, NOW, I'm calling names!

About ten days later, I found out he had been seeing his high school girlfriend. He had kept that part out of the "reasons."

It is now almost two years later. We are divorced. A terrible experience. He had planned this, taking out cash, buying a new car, and he never owned up to me or the children about his girlfriend. He pretended the relationship happened <u>after</u> he left. But the credit card statements revealed a seven-month affair. I had to clean out our house and sell it. Ten years was a lie too. He left so much pain and heartache in his wake. He did leave the whole package. Even the dog.

Name calling is easy for me now: COWARD, literally a SON OF A BITCH, CHEATER, THIEF, LOWLIFE, WUSS, A PIECE OF SHIT, AN EMBARRASSMENT TO THOSE WHO HAD ONCE LOVED HIM THE MOST.

ALL GONE. It would have been easier on all of us if he'd died.

And HE is the victim. HE is angry. At me, the kids. He even told me to give up the dog rather than help pay for her future care. He would not agree to give furniture to the children. He would rather sell it. Sell it? Turned out to be my job to throw out, sell, and donate everything from living there thirty-four years . . . before leaving my beloved home and life.

And HE is still angry.

It is no wonder his adult children have lost their relationship and any respect for him. They tried to communicate with him, although he lied to them about having a girlfriend— and he has twisted the stories of their efforts at communication as well.

The divorce gossip and grapevine has added to the story he tells: he <u>pretended</u> to be happy during our marriage, he hated MY family, I failed him as a wife, he did everything for me and I did nothing for him, I told him to "get out and never come back," our friends who sided with me "drank the Kool-Aid," I took the best years of his life. <u>NOTHING IS ON HIM</u>. Not even the fact that he strayed with his high school girlfriend.

And HE is the still the victim. HE is angry: at me, the kids, and I guess the dog, too. Angry at every turn. Still telling lies, probably hiding income, and never looking back. No remorse shown. No apology given. Not even an inquiry about the dog.

One of my friends said his mother used to say, "A man who can be had, is not worth having."

Touché.

💔

44

At Last Freedom!

Carol from Massachusetts, USA
66 years old
Separated seven years

For our twenty-fifth wedding anniversary, we went to France. That was in April of 2002. After that, it was a downward spiral into craziness. Let me begin. We were married in November of 1977. We were both in our late twenties, college educated, and had good careers. I decided to leave my job and help him develop his, which was the establishment of a dental practice. In the beginning, I ran the front desk, did assisting, cleaned up. It was a lot of work but I loved it, and I felt I was a good asset to the business.

The practice grew and we moved to a bigger office. By that time we had two young children. My husband was a terrific provider. We had fun family vacations, our children were afforded private school, and we were able to send them both to college. As I mentioned, for our twenty-fifth wedding anniversary we traveled, just the two of us, to Paris and then through the French countryside.

About a year later things began to fall apart. He started investing in property in Florida, which meant frequent weekend trips to purchase property. We then bought our own place in Florida, and I was thrilled. As our children were now teenagers I couldn't always leave at a moment's notice to travel to Florida. I didn't feel that it was a good idea to leave teenagers home alone. That's when he started going to Florida alone. He began an affair with a woman there, and it escalated out of control. She wouldn't allow him to leave the relationship.

Once I found out about it, I was devastated but felt I couldn't leave.

I was afraid I'd have nothing, afraid he wouldn't pay for the kids' education, afraid of where I would go. One day, as he was leaving for work, his parting words were, "Your days of a kind and caring husband are over!" He moved out of the house and yet I continued to stay and continued to work in the office! I lived in the marital home with my now college-aged children. He continued to pay for all expenses, the house, and the kids' education. We did try counselling. I went to counseling, but he would not give up his so-called freedom of running around with other women. There were many nights when I'd look up at the full moon and curse out loud for God to just strike him dead or send him a dread disease!

Finally, after years of tolerating emotional abuse, I consulted a lawyer and had him served with divorce papers. Can you believe he was furious? He couldn't believe I would ever do it. I filled out reams of paper work, funnelled financial documents to my lawyer, had the business appraised, and kept copies of every piece of financial information that came across my desk. (And yes, I still continued to work in the office, mainly because it gave me access to his financial dealings, of which there were many!)

Ultimately I decided and urged that we try mediation. We met with a mediator several times and got nowhere because my husband wouldn't negotiate. The mediator said not to schedule another session until the two of us could get together and come up with some sort of plan. So, I tried several times to have him come to the house to discuss division of property, and on two occasions he cancelled because he was extremely fatigued.

Now this was a man who prided himself on staying in great shape. At that point I asked him if he was unwell. He confided that he was having severe back pain and was extremely tired all the time. The children and I urged him to get to his doctor. Last February he was diagnosed with a tumor the size of a grapefruit in the back of his intestine. The tumor had metastasized to his lung tissue, and he died August 23, 2015. Gone at age 65!

The tragedy is that the children buried their father before they were

30 and our grandson was born a month later. I believe that my husband was the victim of many demons. I think his early childhood years were difficult. He was the oldest of seven. His mother suffered several postpartum depressions, and his father had all he could do to cope with a mentally ill wife and seven kids. I believe my husband went through a really severe midlife crisis complete with squandering money and running around with other women.

I believe his time with me was probably the most stable time of his life, but his inner demons won out. As for myself, after he died, I sold the business and some Florida property and consolidated the finances. I have remained in the marital home at least for now. Through all this I have come out financially secure and can help the children, both of whom are married, to set them on a solid path. When I was in the throes of my separation and pending divorce I read *Runaway Husbands* cover to cover and back again many times. It was the only reference that made any sense to me and kept me sane! As for now, I feel strong and happy with myself.

45

Never in a Million Years

Cathy from Calgary, Alberta, Canada
57 years old
Separated three and a half years

November 22, 1974 – November 28, 2012. Thirty-eight years!

We met in a Catholic high school play. He was playing a doctor and I was the lead's mother. He was 17 and I was 16. After the first performance of our play, my European Catholic mother said, "I'd put my shoes under that Dr. Alan Swinford's (Rick) bed any day!" I was totally confused by the comment, and when I figured out that she thought he would be a "real catch," I told her that I was interested in the lead (that's why I had auditioned for the play), not Rick. But that got me thinking . . . hmmm, she must see something I don't. I should open my eyes! I guess I should have had my eyes opened more than I did.

We began dating in November of 1974, and he WAS the best boyfriend any girl (and every girl) could want! He was attentive, romantic, sensitive, kind, funny, and extremely bright. Wow—everything I could have ever dreamed of.

We dated for six years and got married our last year of our undergraduate degrees, in 1980. It was tough financially—but so much fun, because we were so much in love and the envy of every one of our friends. I was getting my bachelor's degree in education and he was getting his history degree, and we were so, so happy. He decided to go to law school in 1981, so we packed up and went to Victoria, where we knew no one—but what a gorgeous place to live. Leaving two teaching jobs behind and struggling to find one teaching job to support us was tough.

After graduating from Victoria, we came back to Calgary to be with family and friends, and Rick accepted an articling position. We knew we would eventually raise a family here, and in 1986 we had the first of our four children. Rick was a successful but very insecure lawyer, always looking to me for support and constant reassurance. That was my job, and I took that job seriously. We had mutually agreed that I would give up my teaching career to raise our four children, and "Mother and Wife" suited me very well. I loved it—I was so happy.

We had the perfect life. A perfect Hallmark family who loved to be with each other and share each other with everyone's friends. Every day he proclaimed that the best part of his day was being "Right here right now around the dinner table with all of you"—the absolute highlight of my day after him kissing me "hello."

It all came crashing down the night before our youngest daughter's 15th birthday party at our home, three weeks before Christmas (and all the gifts had been bought and dinner planned for our usual twenty-plus for dinner), the night our son needed him to help him apply for graduate school, the night before our anxious 19 year old had her very first university exam and our oldest was performing in a play at a well-known professional theatre four hours away in another city . . . and there was a snowstorm.

That morning, he gave me a coffee when I got out of the shower, as I was leaving for the day to help a group of seniors for a field trip, he kissed me goodbye, and sitting on our newly renovated kitchen island was a $200 bouquet of flowers congratulating "us" on the thirty-eighth anniversary of our very first date. Life was good. I was so, so, so happy. I had zero reason not to be. He was happy too, or so I thought. He never gave any indication that he was unhappy. Quite the contrary!

When I got home from the field trip, it was late. He typically taught a legal course in the evening on that day, after his day job as a lawyer. He always called me four to six times a day, every day, to ask me how my day was and what I was up to and to tell me he loved me.

It was 10:00 p.m. and he wasn't home; he should have been at 8:30 p.m.

and I was panicking. I was so worried because he wasn't answering my cell phone calls and hadn't called all afternoon or evening to check in and ask if there would be dinner for him when he got home.

I became ill thinking about what might have happened, fearing the worst—a car accident. As I was sitting on the bathroom floor over the toilet, fraught with nausea, I heard my son come into the house, early and unexpected. I asked him through the bathroom door if he had heard from dad, and he said "Kind of," and I thought, *Oh, thank goodness, he's been in an accident but he can speak—he's OK.*

I heard my son take his two youngest sisters downstairs, and then I heard a bloodcurdling scream come from one of the girls, which was immediately muffled. I came out of the bathroom, and my son was holding an envelope. He looked at me and said, "You need to come upstairs to your room." I kept saying over and over, "Dad's been in an accident hasn't he?" and that's when my life changed for good.

He said, "You need to read this." And I opened the letter from the man who had sent flowers, the scent of the coffee that he had given me that morning and the memory of the kiss we had shared lingering in front of me. He wrote that he was "unhappy and was leaving." The entire letter was a financial accounting, telling what he was paying for. The last line read, "Nothing will change other than I won't be living there anymore. . . . Rick". Not one word of an apology or a reason.

I crumbled to the floor and stayed there for what seemed like weeks, months, years. We had NEVER, EVER had an argument or a fight . . . ever. I had been his cheerleader all of my life. I supported him through so many trials and tribulations, and I was the only person left on this planet who knew him. I took care of his sick and dying parents for ten years, and they both passed away within a year of each other—the last one ten months before he left.

He reluctantly spoke to our 19-year-old daughter, who was devastated after she read her letter saying, "I'm sorry I have to tell you I'm leaving your mom but I'm not leaving you and I'll be an even better dad," because he initially said he wasn't going to be in touch for a couple of weeks and she was worried about him. He actually asked her the night he left on the phone, "Would it have been better if I had jumped in front of a train?" Who asks his child that after he just walked out on her mom?

He was everything to me. He was my purpose, my love, my life, the one I vowed to live with for the rest of my life, who I planned to grow old with and to enjoy what we now could enjoy—our children growing up, becoming independent and leaving the nest, and now it was OUR time . . . and he left.

I thought he was my best friend, but to this day he has NEVER spoken to me or explained what happened or why he did what he did. He never did TELL me he was unhappy, but we met as actors . . . and he obviously played his part very, very well. He told one of the children (not me) that the pretending was killing him—but what pretending? He seemed very. He was home every night for meals; attended every single sporting event the children were involved with, every play, every gig; and we did everything together. We were never apart—ever. I heard my son say to my daughter, "You can't pretend that well for that long."

Movies, theatre, lavish holidays with so much effort, coffee dates, two holidays we had just come back from—one, five weeks before when we had our family pictures done at the spot where we celebrate Thanksgiving annually with our family. My parents adored him as their "son, not son-in-law." My father financially helped us so much to establish Rick in his law practice, and he hasn't spoken to them either. The moment my mother found out, she sat in a chair and cried every day and stopped living. She is barely surviving now—her family gone and broken.

I wasn't a demanding wife. I didn't need all of that! I always said to him, "There are two things that make me happy besides you and my family, and those are windshield wipers that work and a garden nozzle that doesn't leak in my hand when I squeeze the trigger." I used to smile ear to ear when I smelled fresh grass or saw new buds or felt the warm sun on my face. It didn't take much, and now it's all gone.

I can't find pleasure in anything anymore. The smiles are a struggle to put on my face.

The children were and are angry that I couldn't be there for them when this all began because they got their letter from their brother, who read his letter first and then had to tell his sisters and his mother. . . . We all found out together. My poor son had to hand out the letters to his sisters and his mother and watch us all fall apart. What kind of father makes his son do that?

They said it was even more difficult for them because I was crying nonstop here . . . stunned, shocked, and hoping I'd wake up from this nightmare . . . and their dad was crying at his place. Why was he crying? HE CHOSE THIS. HE CHOSE TO BLOW APART HIS FAMILY. He had removed everything from the house that he wanted when I was away on the field trip with the seniors and clearly had this planned for quite some time.

Who does this? This "perfect husband and father" who was never unhappy and loved his family more than life itself just walked away but convinced the children he didn't leave them—only their mother—but our family is gone. The children are on Dad's side. He "left to be happy, which is good for him" is their opinion, and "You're not the only woman some guy has walked out on," said my oldest daughter, to which I explained, "I'm not 'some woman.' I'm your mother and 'some guy' is your father!"

Somehow all the respect that I thought they had for their mom and for their family is gone. He has taken away my parents, my children, my future, and my family and family to come. He said he'd be "an even better Dad," and yet he was a great one when he lived here—and he has outfitted them all with unlimited Visa cards, with trips and dinners and whatever they want or need.

I sit here in my house—lonely—quiet—with no exciting plans for the future. No planning for that trip to Italy we were going to take after I had the ankle surgery I had waited sixteen years for. Plans for us to accompany our children and their children as "Nana and Papa" just as my parents did with us have vanished and are shattered—and we talked about how much fun that would be DAYS before he left at our annual family gathering.

Who can just completely cut out the woman in his life (without even blinking an eye) who was the only one who was there for him for almost forty years and pretend she doesn't even exist and won't attend any of the children's functions if I'm there?

They are angry with ME because they "want their old Mom back." But guess what? She's gone. Not having any support from my children makes it even worse. They are all on "team Dad," and my purpose in life is completely gone. Dad is the hero—he is the happy one— who will do ANYTHING to show them how wonderful he is despite what he's done to his "family," which is now completely broken. I now totally understand the term "a broken family." We are that and more.

NEVER in a million years did I think when I said "I do" to my best friend and future father of my four children and lived my wonderful life with for almost forty years . . . that I would be here in my life at 58.

46

Time Will Be Your Friend, Your Enemy, Your Lover, and Your Confidante

Maria from Seattle, Washington, USA
49 years old
Separated two and a half years

Thanksgiving morning, just before mass began, he put his arm around me and said, "You are the best thing that has ever happened to me. I love you more than I can say." That evening, I flew away for a business trip and I would not return until the middle of the night six days later. If I had known what would happen when I returned home, I know I never would have left.

I returned and the next few days were a whirlwind of work, sports for our 13-year-old twin daughters, and holiday parties. Sunday morning, we were up early and attended a football game party at a friend's home. During halftime, my husband went outside and threw the football with friends. He was always in front of the television the moment the game started, and third quarter began but he didn't come back in. I sent him a text and received three separate replies:

#1 If I tell her, you might have to come get me.
#2 How about after Wednesday?
#3 I am close.

Yes, my husband of seventeen years and three weeks sent me the wrong texts. The texts were meant for the woman who had been chasing him. I questioned it right away, but got a lame excuse. When we got home, I questioned it again. He had three finals on Tuesday and was quite stressed about them, which is why the question to her was, "How about after Wednesday?" as he just wanted to finish those finals.

He asked me to go to our room, where he started to share his thoughts. Immediately upon the start of the conversation, my stomach went into knots. I got heartburn and diarrhea all at once. I had to excuse myself at least twice during our conversation. Well, "Wednesday" became today (Sunday) and about forty-five minutes later, just after six o'clock, he put some of his clothes into his backpack and walked out the door. That night, when I went to bed, my stomach, still in knots, was just not happy. I was cold, had my heated mattress pad turned on, then I was hot. I couldn't lie down because I felt like vomiting; I couldn't sit up because I was too tired. The house was cold.

All through the night, I went in and out of sleep, and each time I woke up my stomach was hurting just a bit more. I found some Tums, ate two of them, slept, ate two more, slept . . . and in between sleeping, oh, the thoughts that went through my head. Anywhere from *Where is he? Who is he with? Is it her? Was this impulse thinking or was he smart and made a wise choice and went to a buddy's house?* And, *Why? Why me? Why us? Why now? Where will this lead us? How do I stay focused until Wednesday? Does she have any clue what she is doing to our family?*

At one point, I got up and texted him. "At this point, I'll be at class on Tuesday to meet her and face it all." Anger. As the night wore on, I tried to focus only on the next few days, not think too far in the future; this was not easy. I could not eat without throwing up. This loss of appetite and inability to sleep well went on for weeks.

When we met again, his wedding ring was off, and in the end he asked for a divorce—all because of a "passion" that he thought he had found. He said he did not know or realize that he was missing or needing this "passion" until it was there. He said that if he had to walk through a door knowing that there was either passion or a bullet on the other side, he would walk through hoping that it was passion.

In early January on a Friday, after a three-hour meeting with legal counsel, an amazing book came into my life—*Runaway Husbands*. I spent another three hours of life engrossed in reading the first 150 pages. Friday night, after these two events, I slept: seven hours straight. Saturday never felt better! I knew at that point I wasn't crazy; other women had gone through this, and I would survive.

Vikki added my name to the Healing Circle in Seattle, and I reached out to the other women on that list and we have nicknamed our group the Runaway Ladies of Seattle. I am the coordinator, reaching out to each new member and always organizing our next gathering. Runaway Ladies has helped all of us who participate; we are each in a different place on our journey, and being able to share experiences helps us along. Runaway Ladies helped me early on, and now I am able to help those who have just begun their journey.

The next few months were living hell. I sometimes just went through the motions. I hired attorneys, found a counselor, and served him divorce papers the day after Valentine's Day. He refused to pay support for his children but demanded to see them, and fought with me time and time again over their welfare. He didn't want to listen and was extremely unreasonable and verbally aggressive, behavior I had never seen before. My legal divorce process was extremely fast (three months) yet financially devastating.

To this day, two years later, he still remains unreasonable and difficult about most things, including our daughters and their needs. I'm thankful he moved out of state, but I continue to struggle with having to be the sole emotional and financial support of our children. My emotional recovery has taken its time. One year of individual therapy, plus another three months of a group therapy exercise, and time have helped me heal.

I'm on the other side and wake up each morning happy. Positive thoughts, positive blogs, excellent friends all have helped me reach that other side. The next step is dating. I've started to date but am not having a lot of luck with that process. I'm sure it will just be more time and all will work out just fine. I dislike that word: *Time. Time* will be your friend, your enemy, your lover, and your confidante.

To this day, I'm not sure what lessons I needed to learn. I can tell you that there is less stress in my life. My girls are stable. I am recovered, positive, and have happiness in my life. I was always a positive, results-oriented person and did not want to become bitter as a result of my husband's choices. I loved being married and having a partner, and I look forward to finding someone new to share my future. Until then, I'll keep getting up every morning and facing the world and all it has to offer. I'll fake it until I make it!

47

"You're So Controlling . . . but Can You Help Me Tell the Kids I'm Leaving?"

Nicole from British Columbia, Canada
46 years old
Separated four years

"I don't love you anymore. I'm leaving on Saturday, and I need you to help me find a way to tell the kids." May 22, 2012, 9:47 p.m. Twenty-three years over.

From 5:30 p.m. to 7:00 p.m. that same night, we had our 6-year-old daughter's teammates over for pizza, since baseball had been rained out. At 8:06 p.m., as I reviewed proofs of a recent family photo shoot, my husband said, "That's a good shot of you and daughter number one. Let's order it." Less than ninety minutes later, he turned the lights off. (It's only now I realize he couldn't do what he was going to do with the lights on.) Of course, it didn't register for the first ten seconds. . . . I must have misheard. . . . What did he say? He loves me. I love him.

"I don't want to look at you." "I don't want to talk to you." "I don't want to touch you." "I don't want to be near you." Although some of that night is now blurry to me, those statements will never be. For the next few hours, he continued his verbal attack. The litany of strange reasons for ending our marriage spewed from his mouth, as I sat there, numb, disbelieving, and confused.

I learned that night I was "a bitch." And that our life "was crap." And that when I hollered at a slo-pitch umpire fifteen years earlier, I had really embarrassed him. And that when I wrote activities on the calendar, or asked him to keep an ATM statement, I was a "control freak." And that I should have known he didn't love me. During the occasional break in his tirade, I tried to clarify with, "Um, you told me yesterday you loved me. . . . One week ago, you and the girls went to a pottery store to make a "We love you" plate, and we ran a Mother's Day run, complete with flowers. . . . You just insisted I buy us a Groupon for Whistler in July. . . . I am not sure how I could have known you no longer loved me."

I'm not sure how long he had been planning his exit or if he intended to do it in such a spectacularly vicious way; all I know is that night remains the second worst of my life, second only to when we did what felt like brutalizing the kids by telling them "Daddy doesn't love Mommy" and that he was moving out.

My husband and I had been together a long time. We dated in high school, split for two years at university, and then reunited, ultimately marrying at 26. Throughout our marriage, I cherished him, and I believed he felt the same. Our marriage was filled with laughter; we were both sports fans and pretty active; we loved movies, TV, books, holidays; we had wonderful friends and family; we went on date nights every three weeks. Our home was filled with photo albums of adventures together over the years, decades of cards and notes between the two of us, his room-consuming comic collection, and most importantly, two amazing little girls, one 6 and the other 4 (who celebrated her birthday the day before what I refer to as "the epic meltdown").

Of course, we had challenges and bumps together. He's an introvert. I'm an extrovert. I've battled depression off and on for years, and he was rock-solid during those times. Both babies were incredibly colicky, with the eldest referred to by the paediatrician as "the most difficult baby I've seen in fifteen years of practice." I went through postpartum depression with both babies; it wasn't an easy time for us, but never did I feel we wouldn't make it. We were also very busy—with graduate education, careers, lots of activities (for us and our kids), and friends. Sex was so-so, good but not frequent enough (which, apparently, was also completely my fault). I admit I was not perfect during the marriage, but I was certainly not deserving of horrible behaviour from someone I trusted.

Just before we had our first baby, the company I was employed at was acquired, and I made enough for us to purchase our home outright, pay off our vehicles, and put aside money for retirement. We made the decision that I would give up my higher-earning career, since we both thought a parent at home would be beneficial. My husband and I often talked about how fortunate we felt to have each other, our financial security, health, and happiness. There was not a single day where I didn't tell my husband I loved him. I too felt loved. Until I was told I wasn't.

While it took me several days of begging him to stay longer than his initial Saturday deadline (as I truly believed he was having a breakdown and that we could work through pretty much anything), the seventy-five days he remained were excruciating. In hindsight, it is clear that he only went to counselling so his good guy image wouldn't be tarnished, and that he could attempt to spin the yarn, "Oh, my wife and I split . . . how sad . . . tried counselling . . . no luck." I call foul here. He had long checked out of the marriage; post meltdown, I discovered e-mails to potential landlords and flirtatious texts to colleagues—all before he ever told me how horrible I was and how he "couldn't wait to have sex with anyone other than" me.

It is now four years later. I have worked very hard to rebuild my life. I'd be lying if I said the way my marriage ended did not alter part of me. I trust less. I worry more. But I will NOT let someone else's behaviour define me. I am raising beautiful, healthy, happy children. I have a challenging career with supportive colleagues. I have a relationship with a lovely man. I have wonderful friends who supported me at my lowest (when I was scared for my children, when I sobbed for days on end, when I was terrified of the future, when I couldn't keep food down), and as I emerged from the fog to take care of the girls and myself physically and emotionally. I'm resourceful and strong-willed and despite being vilified for it, I know that trait got me through the absurdity of being so shockingly dumped!

Unfortunately, because our children are still young, it is necessary to deal with him far too often. He is a loving father, and for that I am grateful. I never malign him to our kids, but nor do I ever say the end of the marriage was a mutual decision. That is not fair to the girls or me. He will one day need to own up to that decision.

Most days are pretty good, but occasionally I am caught back up in the emotion of it all, probably because I still have to deal with shenanigans like attempts to renege on child support, passive-aggressive behaviour, and a new girlfriend with the same name as mine. (Seriously!) It is quite clear that, even four years later, he still views me as the major source of his problems. I look forward to the day when I feel simply neutral about him. I'm not there yet, but am working on it.

48

I Am OK

Virginia from Elmwood Park, Illinois, USA
40 years old
Separated two and a half years

My head is pounding, my body aches. My eyelids weigh a ton. I'm disoriented. Where am I supposed to be? Did I forget an appointment/game/practice/meeting? I'm so exhausted I can't think. What time is it? What day is it?

He left. I walk around in a daze; I'm foggy and unfocused. It feels like I will never ever again be normal. It feels as if no one has gone through this pain that I am in. No one has ever felt this empty, this alone, or this broken. People seem OK, and I am not OK. I'll never be OK.

I pick up the boys from school, hiding in my car so no one sees my tear-stained face, my bloodshot, sunken, swollen eyes and dares ask me what's wrong. All three of the kids come to the car and I say a thank-you prayer that they are all here and safe. I didn't forget one or sleep through pick-up time. I listen as I'm told how I forgot to pack this one's water and that one's permission slip, and did I get the shirt this one has been asking me for? I'm sorry, kids, I'll do better tomorrow. Maybe tomorrow he'll come home. Maybe tomorrow someone will help me get my family back. Tomorrow may be the day I say something magical that will make him realize the mistake he's made.

Tomorrows come, and it's the same thing. The pain is not lessening, the devastation is front and center, always there, following me around like a shadow. With each passing day without my husband, the hole in my soul gets bigger and is bleeding so badly I can't catch my breath. I can't think. I can't sleep or eat or have a conversation without sobbing. I am constantly asking why and never ever finding an answer good enough. I never get a break from myself.

We get home from school, and I smile as I listen to how their day was, make snacks, and get them started on homework. Tell them, with a smile, that I'll just be in my room making a phone call if they need me, and then I close the door and fall on my knees and pray. Please God, let him come home. I stuff my face in my pillow, hoping I'm quiet, and cry until I fall asleep. He's gone, he's gone. Please, God, no. Often times during one of these naps (breaks from reality is what they really are) I open my eyes, shocked that I'm sleeping and scared to death of what may have happened while I was, and I'm frantic. I'm hyperventilating and my heart is about to beat out of my chest.

"Where is your brother?!?" I scream, thinking I have left someone somewhere, alone and afraid. That I've left them like he's left me. That I've abandoned them, like I've been abandoned. Breathe. I start to calm down and realize I made it through another afternoon with everyone in one piece and accounted for. Please, in this brief respite of a nap that I desperately needed, don't let my kids think like I'm weak . . .

Yes, you're going to your game. Yes, you need to study for your test. Yes, I'll take you to the store to get a new notebook. How is this happening? Where is my husband? I can't do this alone.

The weekends that my kids are with him are brutal. I am without my children whom I am supposed to Watch. Love. Protect. Mold. Teach. At all costs. And they are LEAVING. Not because I need a night out, or I'm going on vacation, or they are having a sleepover at Auntie's. There is nothing good about this pending separation from them. The day they leave for the weekend I am in pure hell.

My stomach is in knots all day. I'm short-tempered and impatient. I rush around, trying to get their bags packed early so I can have some last moments with them that aren't chaos. I pack their things in a daze, going over again and again the things they might need. What if they get cold and don't have a sweatshirt or they need more than one pair of socks a day? I over-pack so much that their bags are overflowing. I kiss and hug them and tell them to have fun. I don't cry. I have to be strong. I shut the door behind them and scream to release some of the hurt and anguish. I writhe on my bed in pain; cry myself into a stupor.

The phone is ringing—my family wants to hear my voice or some signal that I'm OK. I'm not OK. I don't want anyone but my husband. I don't want to talk to anyone unless they are going to tell me how to make this right again. I open my eyes and my sister is standing there, willing me to come with her. "Come on, Virg." "Leave me be. I don't want to go. I want to die, just please leave me here." She lifts me out of my bed, and I and my dogs are somehow now in the car on our way to her house. I want to yell at her for taking me, but I can't manage through the tears. I want to tell her to take me back home, but I don't have the energy. I am, as I always am, powerless.

Once I am at her house, my sisters and mom and friends are there to take care of me. The times I'm not sleeping, I'm crying. I drink some wine and talk and cry until I feel like I can live again. Sunday comes, closer and closer to the time when I have to leave the safety I now feel, and I begin the panic again. I am supposed to now go home, alone. Drive down that awful street that I once loved. Open that door that we picked out together. Walk into the empty, depressing house. How am I going to watch my husband drive away from our house when he drops off our kids? How could he not want to be here? Finally, the kids are home, safe and sound. He calls.

The call is instantly hostile and hateful, and my husband's words are vicious and mean. He starts by telling me how much the boys didn't want to come home to be with me. "The kids DO NOT like you, Virginia. You ruined my life, you b----. I've moved on. . . . I'm done with you. . . . You were a horrible wife. . . . You didn't take care of me. . . . You can't love anyone but yourself. . . . You don't know how to love anyone. . . . You are an abuser. . . . Everyone knows what you are. . . . I'm so much happier without you in my life." These post–drop-off calls go on for a long time. They are all horrendous. He drops the boys off, calls a few minutes later, and then rants to me about what a horrible, disgusting, awful person I am; how he is filing for divorce; I will get nothing; I will never be anything without him.

Two and a half years ago, my husband of nearly thirteen years walked away from what I thought was a wonderful marriage. We weren't perfect. We fought, we loved, cried, and laughed. Had countless good times together, building the rock that was our family. One day we are standing on our back porch and he tells me, "I don't want this" (gesturing to the house and me as he emphasizes "this"). I thought he was talking about the dinner I had prepared. I was blindsided, devastated, distraught, broken-hearted, and bewildered.

Within days of him notifying me that he was leaving, my husband went from responsible, dedicated husband and family man to a wannabe twenty-something without a care in the world. He left to find happiness and never looked back. He filed for divorce once he realized I wasn't just going to step aside and let him have this new life he so desired without a fight. Is he happy now? I don't know, but considering the ugliness he still shows me I really don't think so. I don't think he was ever happy, really. I think he faked it until he could no longer hold up the facade. And while this ruse was incredibly unfair to me and our children, I can do nothing to change it. There was not anything I could have said, done, or promised that would have made my husband stay.

Slowly but surely, I began to accept life without him, and now my life is good. I am, for the most part, happy. I still get sad. I still miss the life I had, but I can wholeheartedly tell you that that life wasn't for me. I deserve someone who is true to me and loves me as much as I love him. And you know what? I am OK.

💔

49

To Hell and Back: A Timeline

Lina from Montreal, Quebec, Canada
42 years old
Separated sixteen months

November 2013 – April 2014

Jed takes on a job he has high hopes for, but it turns out to be physically and emotionally soul-destroying. He sinks into himself like he is his own sand trap. It is a depression.

I don't know what to do except take on more of the work at home, make sure the girls are taken care of and that he is free to get some time in the studio (he is an artist and set designer) or to sleep.

I never for one moment think he is unhappy with us.

September – October 2014

He goes on tour with his partners, a husband and wife duo whom I will call Eric and Terri. We've known Terri since high school. Eric is Jed's major collaborator.

He leaves at the beginning of the school year, which is especially trying. Our oldest daughter is struggling with school. We are fighting a lot. Our youngest daughter has no friends. I feel like I am in the eye of the storm, trying to batten down the hatches, trying to keep everyone from drowning.

Jed comes back from tour and he is even more distant. I start thinking that it's me, that he no longer finds me attractive.

I did just turn 40 after all.

November 2014

One day, when we're sitting on the couch having a drink before dinner, I ask him very casually, because I don't really believe it, but I have to ask anyways, "Are you having an affair with Terri?" I tell him I'll only ask him once and that I'll believe him.

He says, "No. Why would you even think that?"

Then I ask him to not let me be one of those women who thinks their marriage is completely fine only to one day find out her husband has been having an affair and is leaving.

He says, "OK, I promise."

December 2014

I buy a sexy (for me) nightgown in order to spice things up. It makes me feel embarrassed and weird, as I have never really understood lingerie (it always felt like gift-wrapping your private parts), but I do it anyways. I am desperate for his attention.

It doesn't work.

February 2015 (Oscars weekend)

Friday morning
Before I go to work, I tell Jed his behavior in the past few months has made me feel really insecure and that I need him to show me more love than less. Then I go to work.

We don't get to talk until late Friday night when in bed he says, "I love you, but I'm not sure I'm in love with you anymore." I am numb. I don't react. I continue doing what has to be done. The laundry. The groceries. Clean the house. Take care of the girls.

Saturday
Annual dinner party with friends. Eric and Terri are there. I know

the minute Terri arrives that something is up. It is a terrible evening.
I drink too much and say sarcastic, harsh things.

Sunday

I am coming home from a walk with a friend. I have the ingredients
for a kale salad that I must make before we head over to our friend's
house to watch the Oscars. He phones me and asks me if I could stop
by his studio on my way home; he needs to talk to me.

He tells me that yes, he has been having an affair with Terri. It started
on tour, right under Eric's nose. While he tells me this, I am looking
at a series of portraits he made of people in his life. Everyone has one
portrait each. Mine is from a photo taken ten years before.

Only Terri has two portraits. They stare at me while Jed tells me he
needs space, he thinks he doesn't want to be married anymore, that
there's a disconnect and that our marriage is in a ditch.

I go home and make the kale salad and we go to our friend's party.
They are waiting for us, after all. I promised a kale salad.

February 2015 – August 2015

He hedges. He speaks in vague notions: "I need space." "There is a
disconnect." "I hate the word 'hope.'" But he doesn't end the marriage.

His "I am no longer seeing Terri" is a lie. They are still seeing each
other. I have to force him to tell me our marriage is over. He finally
does, and I hit him and make him bleed.

But because I made him tell me, I don't believe him. I convince him
that he should at least try to give us a chance. He agrees to meet me
halfway, though he says things like "It's going to take a long time." *A
long time for what?* I wonder. I never get an answer.

We try to go to a marriage counselor. We have two sessions. The first
is very good. She explains to him his own emotional pattern in a way
that makes sense to him. The second session is not so good. I come

prepared with two questions: "How can we bridge the gap between my ease with words and his glacier-like nonverbal process?" and "Why I am here if he is still going to be seeing Terri?"

He remains silent for the whole session.

I leave to go visit our families for the summer. He stays in Montreal. We agree to take a month and then see at the end of the summer if our marriage is really over.

He arrives in August and tells our daughters that he is seeing Terri. He does not tell me first that our marriage is really over.

He just assumes I know.

August 2015 – now

Jed is a master gaslighter and I am only now learning what it means to not engage. Any interaction I have with him leads to him telling me how I also contributed to the end of our marriage, how I am bossy and controlling, and how he simply fell out of love with me.

I am learning to suppress the need to defend myself, to tell him that though I might have contributed to an imperfect marriage, the ending of it was all him. I am learning my own cycle of numbness, followed by the anvil of the chest where the pain is so bad I can't breathe, followed by grief. I wait for it. I feel it. Then I let it go. I meditate every morning, which helps a lot, especially with the accepting and letting go part. I read a lot of self-help books. I am learning self-compassion and how to listen to my instincts again.

I am determined to not let this break me.

Moving Forward

I have taken a leave of absence from my job and am going to take some space to figure out how I want my life to look like, a question I have not asked myself for over twenty years.

Before I do, I am getting a new tattoo to symbolize the ending of this era of my life and commemorate the opening of doors into this new adventure.

It is my time now. I am going to move forward and not look back.

50

Lifted Up

Claudia from Kentucky, USA
59 years old
Separated four and a half years

Just three weeks shy of our thirtieth wedding anniversary, my husband suddenly decided he wasn't happy being married to me anymore and left. He just left out of the blue and never looked back. It was traumatic, to say the least. I would be lying if I said that suicide did not enter my mind. I truly understand now what betrayal feels like.

My husband's mother died the year before, and I noticed that his grief had turned into depression. He was an only child with very few family members. His parents had been first-generation Americans— his mother's family was from Serbia and his father's family was from Ireland. My husband had family in both of these countries, but he did not know them.

I encouraged him to seek help for depression but he was too proud, so he decided to self-medicate. First, he wanted to use money from his inheritance to buy a house that was much too large for just the two us. After I asked him to rethink this purchase, he decided to buy a high-end, red sports car. It was shortly after he felt the power of this car's engine between his legs that he took a mistress. In hindsight, I was able to determine that he left me just two weeks after starting his sexual affair. I don't know when the emotional affair began because I thought he was dealing with grief and depression. When he left, he moved into his mother's empty house (how convenient), which he turned into a bachelor pad . . . the rest is history.

I devoted over thirty years of my life to this relationship and marriage. I took care of both of his parents for the last twenty years of our marriage as their health failed and they eventually died. After his mother died, I became ill. I thought the stress of taking care of her had exhausted me, but what it actually did was reveal a heart and lung disease that I did not know I had—pulmonary hypertension. I spent the better part of the year after her death recovering from heart failure and chronic pneumonia. I had just gotten back on my feet and was excited about taking my life back when he bolted.

When he was packing to leave, I asked him why he was leaving me. He said he wasn't happy and hadn't been happy for a long time. I told him this was all news to me and asked him if he had ever considered talking to me about it. Then he said with great contempt, "You're always sick." I nearly fainted. I realized he was turning on me to justify his behavior. I did not recognize the man talking to me. He lied about me to me! Even the tone of his voice was foreign to me.

He was a stranger standing in front of me. Using my illness was the lowest of lows . . . the blow of that statement to my heart made me realize he was having an affair. He had crossed the line. After he left, I was not able to get out of bed for a week from grief and heartbreak. One week later, when I did get out of bed, I went straight to an attorney's office to file for divorce and never wavered in my effort to end the marriage as quickly as possible.

In the midst of filing for divorce, I learned he had been making financial plans to abandon me for the better part of the previous year. I threw myself into my job in an effort to keep my mind off of the madness. I wept every day for three years. The divorce was over long before I ever stopped crying. I could not get over his betrayal. I could not wrap my mind around his ability to live a lie for thirty years. The old adage "The wife is always the last to know" echoed in my head like a bell.

I received the house in the divorce and little more. I know now that he hid money during the divorce. Unfortunately, my attorney did not represent me well and I came out of this nightmare financially injured. Thankfully, the house is paid off—but now it is all I have. I was recently diagnosed with a rare appendix cancer. This latest blow sent me into a major depression. I am now on disability and unable to afford the house due to medical expenses. As the house continues to need repairs, I am painfully reminded that I will not be able to afford my medical expenses either, so the house must go.

It has taken me two years to dismantle the house, which was like dismantling my life. I cleaned out and threw out over thirty years of memories in an effort to get the house ready to put on the market and my life ready to start over in a new location. I won't be dragging the past with me. In between purging sessions, I have been able to spend quality time with my 97-year-old mother, who is in her last days on earth. The time I've had with her has been priceless.

We've spent our time together researching our family tree. As Mom gets closer to Heaven, we have been blessed beyond measure to learn about the long line of survivors from whom we descend. The way they lived their lives lifted me up. Their life stories spoke to me through the generations, and I realized that I need to do the same for the family I leave behind. I look forward to meeting these strong people someday in Heaven.

My ex-husband and I were never able to have children, but we enjoyed watching my nieces and nephews grow up and start families of their own. We had such fun. We were very close to them. His disgraceful abandonment of me hurt them deeply. My hope is that I will rise above his despicable behavior with grace and leave this world a better place in spite of being injured beyond repair by the one person I loved the most. I will have to "leave him to Heaven" for forgiveness, for I am not able to forgive him.

The ancient Egyptians had a saying: "Speak my name and I live again." This is why they engraved their names on stone monuments for future generations to speak, so that they could live forever. Taking a cue from them, I hope that someday when my nieces and nephews review our family tree with their children and they speak my name and bring memories of me back to life, they will remember me as a survivor and someone in whom they are proud to call family. I hope they will lift me up as I hope to do for them from Heaven should they ever have the need. I pray that they never have a need, but I want them to know they too can rise.

51

You Need to Take Off to Put On

Lorie from Philadelphia, Pennsylvania, USA
59 years old
Separated ten years

Our youngest was a church acolyte on a typical Sunday morning. Ironically, the sermon happened to be about marriage and vows, and I noticed my husband was very fidgety and not relaxed, seemingly annoyed with me. I thought, *Wow, my singing must have been off key today* (Weird feeling #1). After church, I ritually run to a deli for coffee for us while he fuels the car. He said he would get his own coffee (Weird feeling #2). Upon arriving home he went to change his clothes while I read the Sunday newspaper. Eventually he came into the kitchen carrying a duffle bag and announced he was going to the cabin to mow the lawn. Alone. He always asks someone to go along. He never goes for just a day (Weird feeling #3). I questioned the duffle bag, and he said he might have to change if he got dirty. The day progressed and I didn't think about the uneasy feelings I had earlier.

Nighttime arrived and I went to bed. He eventually came home (I don't know if he actually went to the cabin), undressed, and crawled into bed, totally ignoring me. He just lay there with no expression on his face. I repeatedly asked him what was wrong, and he kept saying, "Nothing." I knew there was something wrong, and finally he admitted that he wanted space, that he didn't think he should have gotten married (after twenty-eight years of marriage), that he never experienced living alone, that maybe he was meant to be alone. Then, finally, he wanted to leave! These are words I never thought I would hear. NEVER! I was one hundred percent unaware that we were having marriage problems. One hundred percent!!!

Sure, there were things that bugged me about him, and I am sure (obviously) that I bugged him too. We didn't fight; we were a two-man team, together so long that we instinctively knew each other's needs and desires without having to verbalize them. Wow, was I wrong! How was I going to tell the kids? How was I going to tell my family and our friends? How will I ever walk out the door of our home and face the world? You know, the world of happily married people who will never understand how this could happen to Lorie and Walter. How was I ever going to face the next day?

He started to leave that night, but I begged him to stay. He spent some nights in the basement and some he actually slept at his office. Eventually, he rented an apartment but was shacking up with his mistress at her house. One day, he asked if I would go to a therapist with him. I wholeheartedly agreed, hoping she would help me convince him to return to our home and family. Unfortunately, we had two different objectives. He wanted to learn to better communicate; I wanted him home. We went to a few sessions together and I also went alone.

Not soon after, he bowed out of the couple sessions with the excuse that work had become busy and he couldn't attend anymore. But before he did, his mistress broke up with him, and he sat there with tears in his eyes and actually wanted me to feel sorry for him because he loved her so much! Wait!! I lose my husband of twenty-eight years to said woman and you're shacking up for a year (that I knew about) and you want me to feel sorry for YOU?

This is when I realized that this was not the man I knew. This wasn't my husband. Something had changed in his way of thinking, his morals, and much, much more. His friends all changed, he was drinking excessively, he didn't (and still doesn't) bother with the kids except at his convenience. Our family unit was destroyed because that's what HE wanted, not taking anyone else into consideration. What demon was living in my husband's body?

A midlife crisis had struck him with a vengeance. I could check off practically every item that pertained to midlife crisis in men. In his opinion, I was no longer his mate; he wanted someone else, but he didn't necessarily want to be rid of me. So for ten years I have been a kept woman. Nothing has changed as far as finances in our household. His same weekly paycheck has been deposited in my account. I live in the family home and the summer cottage at the beach. Sounds grand, doesn't it? Well, it is not. In return I may not question his new lifestyle, or life as I know it will no longer be my life.

When I exclaimed that he has ruined my life, he proclaimed that he can easily ruin my future if I don't abide by his "rules." And, I have. For ten long years. Why? Fear. Not fear of him. Fear of the unknown. He was the love of my life; we started dating in high school. He is the father of my children; two of our own, one adopted, and nine foster babies. I hadn't been in the workforce since 1981 because I worked as the bookkeeper for our business for twenty-plus years. He eliminated my position just three years ago. I have lived in the family home for thirty-six years. Fear. Unknown. So hard to communicate why I haven't filed for divorce. (I actually started proceedings that first year, but then I thought things were turning around and I stopped the proceedings.) I honestly don't know how many more changes I could cope with, so I stayed within my familiar comfort zones.

Within these last ten years, I have lost my husband, my family unit, my father, my mother, my job, my dog, which died the day we took our son away to college. I have been to five therapists to help me understand why I can't seem to move forward and why I love/hate this man who destroyed me. I sporadically gain strength and confidence that I can make the changes I need, only to lose it worrying about the "what-ifs" and mostly the unknown. I went to therapy, counseling, doctors, and I read enough books to start my own library. A therapist told me that you need to take off to put on—such simple advise, but also profound.

Thousands of dollars, tears, and as many days later, I repeatedly tell myself those five words (take off to put on), which provide me the strength to move ahead and to stop being manipulated by him. I have found another source of strength. Proudly, I have found new friends! Vikki Stark and all of the contributors to Runaway Husbands. Daily

I read a random paragraph or two, and I get the greatest feeling that I am not alone! This isn't the sisterhood of which I ever thought I would be a part of, but a bond none the less. I am devastated to be a part of WAS, but to read the similarity in our stories and the strategies to gain fuller understanding is just enough to keep me advancing, slowly but surely, to the next phase of my new life.

52

Crepe Myrtle Trees in Bloom

Meredith from Greenville, South Carolina, USA
59 years old
Separated three and a half years

On a seemingly typical Thursday evening in October of 2012, I made salmon croquettes for my husband. Using my cast-iron skillet brought back cherished memories of girlhood. Turning each patty in a clockwise motion I mused. "Third time's the charm." I had tried frying my mom's recipe twice to unappetizing results, but this time I felt triumphant. The familiar aroma of the sizzling croquettes filled the kitchen. The sharp ring of the phone brought me out of my thoughts. Just like clockwork, "Honey, the six-thirty conference call has run over so I'll be late for dinner."

Dinners were decidedly lonelier these days since Maxine had moved out for her freshman year of college. We loved cooking meals together, since she had taken a culinary course in high school. I was determined to maintain our traditional evening meal as we watched Brian Williams with the *Nightly News* on the small television in our kitchen. We made light conversation about Dave's work as we ate, and he complimented the meal in that he knew it was difficult for me to cook without Maxine by my side.

Having an empty nest hit me hard. I retreated to my office after dinner to call my girls. Later, hungry for something sweet, I stepped back to the kitchen to grab an ice-cream sandwich from the freezer. Dave called out from the sofa, "Is everything all right with the girls?" "Yep," I called back, "Just chatted about things going on with Michael" (the oldest). As I unwrapped the frozen snack, but just before taking the first bite, I heard an unusually stoic voice from

Dave: "Meredith, can you come here? We need to talk." I couldn't remember a time in our marriage that he actually wanted "to talk," so naturally I was anxious as I entered the room and felt a thick, tense atmosphere.

He was sitting in his usual place on the sofa—but without his laptop. I knew immediately this was serious. The seconds seemed like hours as I studied my husband's face. "I need some time away," he stated. Those seemingly innocuous words dismantled the life that we knew. After that conversation, I would never sit beside my husband on that sofa again. When I asked if there was someone else, he replied, "No, there is no one else. In time you will realize that." He moved out within a week.

I valued my marriage and prided myself for being a good wife and mother. It's hard to explain the gravity of abandonment and trying to make sense of living with a person almost twenty years, over 7,000 days, and all the wonderful life events including the birth of our daughter. We were a tight-knit family. How could he just leave?

The months before he moved out were difficult. He was irritated and unhappy most of the time. One evening in particular, Maxine and I had prepared dinner as usual and heard the garage door open. Dave entered in his starched, button-down shirt and tie. He immediately went to the sink, noticing pots and pans. "What is all of this? Why do I always have to clean up?" This just didn't make sense and was almost comical. How could we cook without pots and pans?

Now I realize his change in personality and attitude was because he was planning to leave. He was typically funny and charming in the earlier years. In retrospect, I can almost pinpoint the time frame. It was shortly after the holidays that his personality changed. He began trying to change our plans for a trip to Europe we promised our daughter for her high school graduation and looked very distant and lost in the photos.

It seemed our family had just settled in to our new home. Dave and I spent so many years dreaming and researching. It was a partnership and labor of love. We combined our styles to result in a very eclectic dwelling that we were proud of. From every angle, the architecture was interesting and balanced.

The months that followed the abandonment announcement were lonely and fearful. Living alone in our home that we built together was unbearable. I would lay on the couch, unable to move from depression and fear. Every square foot of the house reminded me of him and our life together.

Our marriage was pretty wonderful the first ten years; however, he was always a workaholic. It was a problem in our marriage the first few years, and then when the economy changed and people lost their jobs, I changed my attitude and felt the need to be more understanding about the late hours and work at home. I decided to give him space, so I didn't complain about his isolation and separate bedrooms, hoping that we could work on and try to rebuild our marriage to what we once had. I was neglected to the point that I didn't ask for or require his attention, hoping that someday it would get better. Our life had become increasingly isolated, with little social interactions. I don't think it was intentional, but I felt emotionally abused and beaten down.

Theories of why my husband abandoned me:

1. Gradual lack of communication. Work was priority. He felt more comfortable at work than at home. He just doesn't want to be married and would rather be alone.
2. Fear of intimacy, especially with empty nest after our daughter moved away to college.
3. Midlife crisis and health-related insecurities.

I still really miss our life as a family and my home. On a beautiful spring day like today, my thoughts go back to how our crepe myrtle trees must be blooming and how the loropetalums probably need to be trimmed. One of the saddest days of moving out of our home was letting go of my yard tools—knowing that I wouldn't need them in my low-maintenance apartment.

Moving forward—It's been three and a half years, and my head has been so full of obsessive thoughts of why that I am just fully realizing that I am dealing with years of emotional neglect. I refuse to be a victim, even though I feel betrayed. I will try to hold on to the good memories of the years of love. I am blessed and grateful for the support of family and friends that has enriched my life. I do not want to give up on finding a meaningful relationship.

This life change has revealed many blessings. My family relationships are even richer. My daughters and siblings have been my best friends through all of this. I have found a community of strong, wonderful women whom I count as friends and who display incredible resilience. Some, I've found, are in a similar situation. The road to recovery is long, and I feel that healing should be a priority. There are so many people with challenges who live life to the fullest. I am ready to get unstuck and embrace my new independence.

53

Grateful for this Life Experience

Lief from West-Vlaanderen, Belgium
46 years old
Separated five years

End of February 2011, I was left on my own. And today, June 2016, I am happy to stand on my own. Next week, I start rehearsals with an international group of four young, talented contemporary dancers; a childhood dream becomes true. Taking part in the creation of *Le Terrier*, opening in Brussels in Theatre Les Brigittines, October 2016. I AM SO HAPPY!!!

I have gone through difficult times. My husband left me for a woman (a friend of close friends) who I really did not fancy. In autumn 2010, she made advances to him on Facebook. I confronted him with it and he comforted me by saying that he would take care of it. And I believed him. On our thirty-fourth wedding anniversary in November, he gave me flowers and a card with the text "Another 34? I surely do!"

End of February 2011. I found out about his relationship with her because he left his mobile phone at home when he was at work. There was a message, and I checked to see if maybe it was important. She sent the message. I discovered that he got a lot of messages from her. The earth under my feet disappeared. I felt in my stomach that the tie with him broke, and in my head I saw my life had taken another road.

I phoned the wife of another close friend to ask if she knew about the affair. She answered, "No. That is not possible. Maybe she is stalking him!" But then she asked her husband and he knew about it. They told him the day before, he said. When my husband came home, he said to me with a firm voice, "OK, now you know. I respect you as a good person, but I don't see you as a partner anymore. So let's talk about it." I couldn't talk because I was crying all the time. He left.

The weeks after, we met a few times to arrange the divorce. And I looked for another place to live. I always wanted to live at the seaside and soon found an apartment with a sea view to rent. When I told him that, he asked if he could visit me. I said, "Yes of course." I was confused, angry, and sad, but I wanted us to stay friends. Then, on that occasion, he told me that she was very ill. I was compassionate and agreed that she needed him and that we would only have contact by mail to arrange things. During this period, he began to react with hostility. He was not my friend anymore.

Did I get support from other common friends? No, except from two couples who are still friends with me. The others were supporting the new happy couple. Luckily, I had good friends of my own and I knew that I could make other friends in my new hometown. So I cut the contacts with people who said, "Why are you still sad?" "She is such a warm, loving woman!" "You react too emotional." "I know why he left you, but I won't tell you because he told me in confidence."

And I started a new life.

Oh, it was hard, very hard. I tried to concentrate on myself and my new situation as much as possible. I loved my job and got great support from my coworkers. I went to art class, where I met new people and discovered my creative talents. And I started therapy because it is too hard to walk the road alone. But you can't cut the past. It pops up in dreams, in memories, in situations, in photos and posts on Facebook, in music. It is uncontrollable. It is falling into despair, crawling up again. It is hard work, it takes time. And you don't know how long it will take.

I decided never to take care of another grown-up as I did with my ex-husband for all these years. And I forgave myself for doing it. I was only 18 when I fell in love with him. But even at 60, I fell in love with a young man who was needy. He had no work, no place to live.

I told a good friend what was happening, and she warned me: "Do not to give up your life of freedom for this guy." Instead of suppressing my feelings I asked her to stand by me. I wanted to live through all my feelings, longing for him. I wanted to know what happens to me when I fall in love. As Odysseus did, I tied myself to the post of my ship and listened to my Sirens. It gave me insights in my way of projecting my own needs and dreams on a lover.

In the winter of 2013, I almost collapsed. I felt horrible. I was so down and sad with my life. Thinking negative all the time. How could this have happened to me? Wasting almost forty years of my life for a man who dumped me so cowardly. Why did I not leave him before because I knew he had lied in the past? He'd acted horribly and aggressive before. I gave my daughters a bad example. All the time the most horrible memories and scenarios in my head. Day and night. I didn't want to live anymore. I didn't try to commit suicide but tried to hold my breath. Impossible, of course. Your body forces you to breathe.

My therapist noticed that I was too sad. I went to a good psychiatrist. He diagnosed a severe depression and gave me medicine. My body reacted well, but it took two months after starting the cure to feel better. And in this time I decided to answer an ad for participants in a dance project for the summer of 2014. I didn't know if I would be strong enough, but I was. And it was such a healing experience. I could be and was appreciated and loved totally as myself.

And I knew that I had grown. That I don't need a partner to care for to feel happy. That I am at the happiest when I support and care for myself. And that love comes in many ways.

How do I live my life now? I don't have to work anymore because since October 2015; I am retired and have a pension that I can live on. I live quietly and in my own way and in my own way. Most of the time I am alone and I like it. Enjoying my home as my playground. I go to art class and participate in art projects. I have only really good friends. I have a good and open relationship with my two wonderful daughters and two amazing grandchildren. I now really take care of myself. Accepting myself as I am with the good and bad aspects of my personality. Fond of my own company.

What has also helped me is meditation and listening to mantras, watching and listening to the sea. Reading a lot of books. I feel especially grateful to Julia Cameron for *The Artist's Way: A Spiritual Path to Higher Creativity*, Clarissa Pinkola Estés for *Women Who Run with the Wolves: Myths and Stories of the Wild Woman Archetype*, John A. Sanford for *The Invisible Partners: How the Male and Female in Each of Us Affects Our Relationships*. And to you, Vikki, for your work.

I hope my ex-husband is happy now with his life. As much as I am now.

This is my story for now. Not ended but already happy. Going with the flow, with the waves. I will not drown, because I know I can rely on lifesavers, inside and outside myself.

54

No Plan, No Explanation, No Relationship after Twenty-Six Years Today

Sara from Vancouver, British Columbia, Canada
49 years old
Separated ten months

"I'm done," my husband said to me in the car on the way home from the airport. He had picked me up after I had been visiting my widowed father on the other side of the country. He looked strange, was vibrating and smelled of booze in the middle of a Monday afternoon. In the thirty minutes it took to get home, he imploded twenty-six years together and twenty years of marriage.

I was shell-shocked, living a nightmare, but I kept a clear head. I said we would work on it, but he wasn't interested. His language was cold and harsh and his delivery detached and arrogant. He told me he didn't love me. When I asked if there was someone else, he fiercely told me, "Maybe."

After we arrived home, the deed done; he went up to his home office and proceeded to work like it was any day. I finally got him to speak to me, and he stood in the kitchen staring at his Converse sneakers while I asked him to explain, begging for our marriage. He told me it was too much work. Marriage shouldn't be work. When he did look at me it was with so much contempt and disgust, like I was physically repulsive to him.

I had no idea that this was coming. We had no children, but our lives were full and busy. We had good jobs and hobbies. My husband was a free spirit who seemed to do exactly what he wanted. He wrote and played music, practicing at home and playing in his favourite bar. He traveled regularly for work. We took great trips and had fun together. It never occurred to me that he was not happy or didn't love me or wanted out for a "long time," as he informed me. We had our rough spots, but I thought we were best friends. We had taken a great trip to celebrate our twenty-year anniversary two months before the Big Day.

The blindsiding was the worst thing. Honestly, I can't imagine handling such an important event in a poorer way. He hit me with cliché drivel—told me he needed a "jolting change" because he was "broken inside" and saying things like he didn't see me "that way" and that he would rather die alone than be with me. As he had no plan to leave the home, needing support, I went to a friend's house. He didn't follow me to the door, just stood there defiant and glad to be rid of me. So, essentially, I was left without being left.

That was the last time I saw or spoke to him. There were a few texts and e-mails in the days and months ahead ("I don't expect you to understand," one read), but that was pretty much it. Birthdays and Christmas went unmarked as though we never knew each other.

To say I was a mess in that time is an understatement. I was able to work because I couldn't afford to leave my job, but that was about it. I was consumed by my lack of understanding of what had happened. Why didn't he tell me how he was feeling before it had been too late? How did this happen and how did I not know? I felt ugly and old—a reject and a failure. I wasn't even worth an explanation. But then he had another woman. I punished myself by not eating and quickly lost fifteen pounds, went on antidepressants, Ativan, and sleeping pills. I thought of suicide nonstop. It was the only thing that gave me control in my life. There were counselors and finally a therapist who helped me as much as he could. I was looking for closure, but there wasn't any and never would be.

I was left in a 114-year-old house with rats and broken pipes and appliances, wondering when he would stop paying his share. Three days into the New Year, I was served divorce papers late on a Sunday night. I was in my bathrobe, with no access to counsel and no way to interpret the papers, which appeared to be asking for spousal support and rent and for me to sell the house as quickly as possible. We would meet in court to divide our assets. He was in such a rush. The papers had been filed before the holidays and only a few months after "the end." He wasn't wasting any time.

I put the house up for sale a week later and sold it completely alone. My friends were amazing and came from across the country to help me in the ensuing months as I cleared away all our possessions. Everything happened so fast and I was responsible for it all. I sold the house, bought a new home, and was on my way to divorce. He had a clean getaway. Didn't lift a finger. He had simply walked out of his life.

It's now ten months since it happened, and the dog and I are settled into a new home that we love. Money is tight, but I get by. My friends and family are incredible people who have stood by me when I raged at the world. There never was and never will be responsibility or accountability on his part for what he put me through, but he has always been good at compartmentalizing his feelings.

I, on the other hand, am not. I have faced this thing head-on, and it has almost destroyed me. But the point is, it hasn't. While thoughts of failure and lack of understanding still plague me, the voices are muted and I now know that this wasn't about me but about him. It's always been about him.

I realize that things are easier because we don't have kids, but in some ways it's harder. Once it's done, it's done and you don't have any connection. It's tough to spend half your life with someone and then, in one thirty-minute conversation, it's over and you are nothing to one another. As for him, I understand that the relationship with the "maybe woman" turned out to be not what he thought and never went anywhere.

Time is a healer, as is surrounding yourself with people who care and respect you. But alas, nothing really changes what happened. It stays with you and alters your world view. I am not the same person. I am not at peace with how my marriage ended, and I am embarrassed to be a divorced person. I took this commitment seriously, but we can't control others—only the dignity and respect we show ourselves. I deserve better and I will get it.

55

Always Keep Your Eyes on Your Honey and Your Money

Laura from American Canyon, California, USA
59 years old
Separated eight years

I had the perfect, middle-class life—a hard-working, educated husband; two great kids, a 10-year-old boy and 13-year-old girl; a two-story California mission-style home in Napa Valley; a successful career; close friends and family nearby; and never had to worry about money. One Saturday night in January 2008, my husband, Ken, went to his second job as an ICU registered nurse on the night shift. I sat down at the computer to catch up on my e-mails. That was the night my life changed forever!

My husband had left his e-mail open and I thought, "I'll just see if he has heard from any of his family members recently, etc." I skimmed through his inbox and saw that he had ordered a Valentine teddy bear in February 2007. I thought, *Gee, I don't remember getting a teddy bear for me or Emma* (our daughter). When I highlighted the entry, a teddy bear wearing a leather outfit, sitting on top of a motorcycle, was carrying a card reading, "Dear Stephanie, I want to be your lover boy!" (Certainly, this was not meant for my daughter or me!) I thought this must be a mistake. This can't be from "my Ken." I looked at the name and address of the order, and to my "shock and surprise," it was from "my Ken."

I did some further digging into his e-mail, and "girl," was I in for a surprise. In a nutshell, I discovered that my 64-year-old husband of twenty-one years was sending and receiving e-mails from a 27-year-old nurse's aide who was a high school drop-out, was already divorced, and had two small children. I almost fell off my computer chair when I discovered that Ken paid for boat insurance on a brand-new 2006 Air Warrior ski boat and bought a 2007 Ford F-350 pick-up truck, fully loaded, to haul the boat! I didn't even know what a Ford F-350 looked like!!! And I thought, *We're not boat people. This couldn't be happening to me!!!*

Then I started rummaging through a box of bills on the floor next to the computer. I discovered two different cash loans; one for $10,000 and another for $25,000. Then, I discovered two credit card statements, one for $2,500 and another for $10,000, and of course, they were already maxed out. Upon closer examination, the charges were for Victoria's Secret, Sephora, and restaurants, for places located outside the county. Nothing that was familiar to me.

Then I came upon the credit card charges for Comfort Inn and the Hilton Hotel in nearby communities. And at that point, my heart was very heavy and sank to the bottom of my gut. I was in awe!!! I said to myself out loud, "I can't believe it! Ken is having an affair! And giving away all of our money!" Oh yeah, I forgot to mention that I noted on his checking account that he was making $500 cash withdrawals every ten to fourteen days, and later discovered that he was giving this money to his girlfriend.

It just made me Sick! My immediate thoughts at the time were, *How could he do this? Ken was my best friend before we got married. I'm his second wife and had been faithful all these years! When was he doing this? Where was I when this was all going on? Was I that blind?*

Of course, I was frantic; stayed up all night, researching every piece of paper I could find, and reading every e-mail. I can clearly remember how my heart was just burning inside of me. I was in total disbelief! I have two young children. What do I do now? Should I confront him in the morning when he comes home or pretend I don't know? What do I tell my two older brothers, my older sister, and my mother, who had been against me marrying a divorced man who was twelve years older and had a 12-year-old child from a previous marriage (and I was brought up Catholic?). Interestingly, I did not cry, but I was angry and disgusted.

When he came home at 8:00 a.m., I asked Ken how his night was. He said, "Fine, busy." I replied, "Well, I guess you better plan on working a lot of those extra night shifts to support that girlfriend you have." He replied, "What girlfriend?" And I just laid into him verbally, cussing and calling him names while trying to keep my voice down because my children were sleeping upstairs. "Don't you lie to me, you SOB! I accidentally came across your e-mails you left open and discovered that you have been screwing someone and giving away all of our money!!! Are you crazy? You're lucky we don't have a gun, because I would be tempted to kill you right now! But, then again, I'm not going to go to jail for your indiscretions!" "How old is she? In her 40s?"

He replied, "No, she's 26." "What? 26? She's younger that Aubree" (Ken's older daughter from his first marriage who was 33 years old). "I suppose she is some skinny nurse you work with at the V.A." He replied, "No, she's a nurse's aide and she weighs 260 pounds." I replied, "What, she's bigger than me! Are you nuts?" He replied, "I knew I should have told you a long time ago." I said, "How long has this been going on?" Ken said, "About two and a half years." "Oh," I sighed. "Unbelievable."

At this point, my young son, Kenny, came down the stairs and said, "Mom, are you OK? Was Dad cheating on you?" Then I felt my heart come out of my body. I just wanted to die right there. The last thing I wanted was for my children to get hurt and something like this to affect their lives forever. I told Kenny, "Honey, Daddy has made some mistakes and everything is going to be OK. Go back to bed." (Of course, he went to the kitchen to pour himself some cereal and milk.) Ken said, "I'm really tired right now. Can we just talk about this later? I've been up all night working," as if we were just talking about something casual.

So, later that night we talked and talked. He decided to end the relationship with her the following Saturday at five in the morning. And, of course, I followed him and confronted her! I was calm and told her, "You know, Stephanie, people get killed over things like this."

She started crying while sitting in the driver's seat of her new Volvo S60. (Oh, that's right, Ken bought her that too!) She was nothing special to look at—plain face, long dirty-blond hair, and overweight! Ironically, I actually felt sorry for her. Shortly after, I filed for a divorce. My lawyer filed for spousal and child support over Memorial Day weekend 2008, right after Ken moved out and four months after my discovery.

Again, I was devastated! What do I tell the kids? They knew what happened and what their dad did shortly after I made my discovery in January 2008. My solution: I told Emma and Kenny that their dad made some bad decisions and that he needed some time alone to think things out. I will admit I was angry and sad, disappointed mostly because I was supposed to be "the younger woman" in his life. How could I fail at my marriage?

Epilogue

The last eight years have turned out to be very interesting. I can tell you this: I stayed separated all of these years. After five years of my case being on the books in the courts, I dismissed the divorce proceedings against my husband.

You may ask Why? I did not want to lose my health benefits, since he was retired military, and it cost me nothing, as well as for the children. I received almost $4,000 a month in support without a fight, until they reached 19 years old and he retired from his primary nursing job. I did not speak to Ken for a year, but I never kept him from seeing his children. I always kept it cordial for the benefit of my kids.

He always had access to the children, spent time with them, and attended all of the graduations and celebrated their birthdays with them. My main focus: I had to be strong for my children and show them not to give up in times of adversity. I thank God that I am a registered nurse myself, in critical care, and was able to continue paying my bills and have money to pay the mortgage, children's expenses, etc. I worked overtime on-call, sold items on Craigslist, and saved every penny that I could. Many times I wondered, *How do women manage who don't have a career or job that they can fall back on?*

Dating other men was not of any interest to me. All I could think about everyday was being there for my kids! And, I decided to make it a point for Ken and me to get along over the years. (He lives about an hour away in Sacramento, in a trailer on his older daughter's property in the country.)

Here's the surprise ending: About one and a half years ago, Ken, now 71, came over to visit the kids and, afterwards, wanted to talk to me. He realized the grave mistake he made and asked for my forgiveness. I was taken by surprise. "Are you asking for us to get back together?" He said, "Yes. We always got along. I don't know why I did what I did." My reply, "Well, we just have to take this slowly. And figure out how we're going to do this."

It's been exactly eight years, over the Memorial Day weekend, my "now" 22-year-old daughter Emma graduated from San Francisco State University with a B.S. in health education, with all of us at the AT&T Baseball Park. Emma told me on Sunday evening when we were alone, "Mom, I really like it when we are all together as a family." Even though I am now 59, I replied, "I know honey . . . I'm working on it."

Words of Hope

My advice to other women:

1. Be strong. Don't give up. You have to be there for your children and other loved ones.
2. Don't start drinking and feeling sorry for yourself. If anything, start taking better care of yourself. Work out. Exercise. Eat healthy!
3. Be cordial and try to be civil to each other, especially if you have children. Fighting just increases tensions with each other and can severely affect the children's upbringing and future, psychologically and physically. (We started family counseling last fall. I would recommend counseling sooner; but better late than never!)
4. Keep your eyes on your "Man and your Money," or better stated in this day and age, "Your Honey and your Money." I

realized I did not give my spouse enough attention—always coming home late from work, working extra shifts, etc. Still, it is no excuse for what he did, but I feel I need to take some ownership of what happened, as well.

5.   Interestingly, I am actually at peace right now in my life. I like my independence. I see Ken once every three to four weeks, with or without the children. I'm in no hurry for us to live together. And, my time is my own. (He set up a camping trip for the four of us in late July, where we will be with other members of his side of the family.)

6.   Most importantly, I have learned to forgive. Not forget . . . but to forgive, in order for me to have peace in my life. And, as a result, I'm not in pain anymore. Time does heal, and the hurt has gone away. And, I'm especially proud of my children and myself, because we have always kept it together and not fallen apart.

7.   Act "smart on your decisions" and not "reactive"! My motto was always "Don't get even . . . get AHEAD!" Remember, you want to be mindful of any extra expenses you may incur by making quick, emotional, and maybe irrational decisions. (The lawyers always win. I spent about $16,000 in attorney fees, just to end up dropping the case after five years because my spouse and I decided we would work together and save money for our children.)

8.   Take it one day at a time. Get professional counseling. Talk to close friends and family for support. And make decisions on how you, the victim, feel. Don't let others tell you what to do . . . "Get a divorce," "Get rid of him," "Start dating other people," etc. Do what you feel is best yourself and for your family. Put yourself and your kids first!

9.   Make time for self-meditation, and ask for spiritual support, in whatever style you are comfortable and accustomed to in your life.

56

Neighbors—More than Friends

Katherine from Albany, New York, USA
47 years old
Separated two years

My life as I knew it imploded the winter of 2014. Like a bad storm that blew in unexpectedly, I never saw it coming! I was left totally devastated and struggling to care for my three young children and hold down my teaching job.

My husband and I had been married for fifteen years and had been a couple for twenty. We had built a wonderful life together. We lived in a beautiful home that we built together in a neighborhood where we had made friends who felt like family. To complete the picture, we had brought three beautiful children into the world. My husband and I had always been great friends who rarely fought. He was still quite affectionate toward me and told me he loved me daily. I saw myself as very fortunate and was still very much in love.

One day, out of the blue, my husband announced that after our son's 8th birthday party that evening, he would be meeting some work friends for a movie. Surprised, as he never went out without me, I asked what movie they would be seeing. He told me the name of a movie we had just seen together the week before. The fact that he never went out with friends and was planning to see a movie he had already seen was unsettling.

Later that night, when he had returned home and was in bed asleep, I decided to look through his phone. I needed to relieve my fears. I assumed I would find nothing to be concerned about and put this nagging doubt to rest. I snuck downstairs and found his phone. When

I turned it on, a text instantly appeared on the screen. My heart sunk as I read the words all wives dread to find, "I love you so much!" The nightmare had begun.

After hours of searching his phone and using reverse phone book on the Internet, I discovered he was having an affair with one of our neighbors! I found an endless call log and texts that seemed like a secret language; one he never used with me. Messages such as "L U" and "L U 2" and "Can't wait till it is just u and me." I was crushed! He had her in his contacts under George Glass, the name of the fictitious boyfriend of Marsha Brady! It was a joke to him! She was actually a married woman with two very young boys who lived only houses away. A woman who had chatted with me at neighborhood parties, acted like my friend, all the while sleeping with my husband.

I woke him and confronted him with my revelation. His unexpected response was, "People say life with young children goes quickly. I just don't see it. This life isn't for me. The house, kids, family, marriage. I just can't do it." He went on to say there was something wrong with him and maybe he needed help. He explained that he felt nothing. He had said, "Men just don't walk out of their families, but I feel nothing." I was in shock, as my life began to unravel.

That day I sobbed harder than I ever had, so hard that my whole body shook. My husband explained, coldly, that he loved me but wasn't "in love" with me anymore. I desperately grabbed at pictures of our children, holding them up to him and begging him not to leave us. I grabbed a picture off a shelf of him and me a decade before, hugging happily at a wedding. I begged him in tears to look at that picture and not do this. He looked at me, totally detached, and said, "That is not us anymore." I was destroyed. I begged him to go to marriage counseling, saying at least we could then tell the kids we had tried. He outright refused, saying, "Blame it on me. I just don't want to." When I fearfully asked if he wanted a divorce, he looked me square in the eyes and said yes, with no hesitation.

I was in absolute disbelief. This man had acted utterly happy and content with his life only a day before. The night prior he had reminded me to finalize our reservation for our upcoming vacation to the ocean with the kids, and when asked about possibly getting family portraits done, he had said, "Schedule it!" In the night, he had held my hand as we slept. Now when I tried to hold him, he turned away, as if he didn't want to be disloyal to his married girlfriend. Where had my husband gone?

We began talking of a divorce and splitting up our life. I cried endlessly as he sat totally dry-eyed. He then sat the children down and with little emotion told them he had done something terrible to Mommy and couldn't live here anymore. I followed him as he went up to our bedroom. He seemed to look through me, repeating over and over, "This is the first day of rest of my life. I must be strong. I must be brave." I was devastated and totally baffled. He was destroying his family and yet was giving himself a pep talk.

My oldest son, then 11, lay on the floor of his bedroom in a fetal position, sobbing as his father drove away that day. Like myself, our children never saw this coming. We had rarely fought, so the kids had been given absolutely no warning that their life and security was about to crumble.

The pain was palpable. I cried endlessly for months. I dropped thirty pounds quite quickly, as I went days without remembering to eat. The pain of this abandonment felt more like the grieving of a death. I questioned if his death would have actually been easier than him abandoning us.

He moved into an apartment and instantly began putting up framed pictures of him and his girlfriend. He hung up plaques on the walls that read "Faith" and "Hope." My children, then 6, 8, and 11 were utterly confused and deeply hurt.

When I thought things couldn't get any worse, his girlfriend's marriage ended and my husband moved back into our neighborhood, only houses away, with her and her two young boys! My children hadn't even met her yet and he was living with her! I was so embarrassed and humiliated for myself and my children.

It was at this point I realized I needed to begin the horribly slow and painful process of moving on. I gave up any hope of reconciliation and filed for the divorce he so eagerly wanted. I began to accept that my life had not turned out as I had so carefully planned. I had no other choice but to go on. I slowly became stronger and realized I could get by without him.

I am now at the two-year mark and though I'm far from healed, I know I am on my way. I have proven my own strength. I survived! I have learned that it truly isn't how many times you get knocked down, it is how many times you get back up.

57

Here Today, Gone Tomorrow

Sarah from Pardeeville, Wisconsin, USA
36 years old
Separated two years

We had just celebrated our five-year anniversary; our beautiful daughter was going to be 3 in a few weeks, and I had found out only weeks earlier that I was pregnant with our second child. Everything was heading in a good direction for us—we were happy! But life is so unpredictable. I often remember these events in my head and am still in shock—How did this happen?

My ex-husband, Shaun, and I had been looking at houses for the previous several months; we had met with a realtor and the bank only a week before his abrupt departure. I absolutely didn't see this coming. My ex-husband took me on a surprise anniversary getaway also only a few weeks earlier. Then on March 11, 2014, we went to the doctor's office for my second ultrasound; I was nine weeks pregnant. That is when we were told there was no fetal heartbeat. We were both tearful and heartbroken. My ex-husband held me, told me he loved me and that we would get through this together.

The next several days were a blur of tears and starting to get myself back together physically after the loss. My ex-husband began to withdraw; I assumed it was his way of dealing with the loss. Six days after the miscarriage and D&C, I scheduled an appointment for us to see a counselor to help deal with the grief of the loss. I explained to her the grief of the sudden pregnancy loss we had experienced in the last week. She had kind words and reassuring advice. She then asked my ex-husband how he was handling it. (He was even more withdrawn at this point, wouldn't sit by me in the waiting room, and sat with his arms crossed in a chair opposite from me when were with the counselor.)

I was so confused between the miscarriage, the change in hormones in my body, and my husband's recent out-of-nowhere bizarre behavior. My ex-husband opened his mouth, and I will never forget his words or the sound of his voice at that moment: "I am only here to dissolve my marriage with the least amount of impact on our daughter." The counselor explained to him that after such a traumatic week, this wasn't the best time to make any major decision or changes. My ex-husband then said something to the effect of "Is there ever a good time to ask for a divorce?" He exchanged some more words with the counselor, but I was in shock. . . . I only vaguely heard anything. All I could think was, *Is he really saying this? Why is he doing this now? This is so out of character for him.*

Before I knew it, he stood up and left. The counselor was so kind and stayed and talked with me for another hour, asking questions like, "Were you having trouble in your marriage?" All I could think was, *NO, we have plans to go look at houses this weekend. He had been kissing me and my pregnant belly good night since I found out I was pregnant.*

After that moment, things quickly fell apart. I did try to speak with Shaun, explaining that our problems aren't unsolvable and there is too much to lose by getting a divorce. He was now icing me out, telling me I was a bully and he wasn't going to take it anymore. I remember thinking, *What are you talking about? If you were this upset, how could you never mention it to me?* Within three days of the appointment with the counsellor, he was e-mailing a shared parenting schedule for our daughter.

This whole event was such a nightmare; I am still so disappointed that he did this just days after my miscarriage, that he dissolved our marriage without even talking with me or letting me know this is what he was thinking or that he was wanting to go. Just the disregard and disrespect to me was so painful to my soul. As the days went by, I was surprised how I managed to function.

I was so blessed to have such great co-workers, friends, and family who are so understanding and kind. I remember falling asleep between my parents in their bed, crying desperately, missing my daughter (who until this point I had maybe been away from for six nights) and the life I once had. Their comfort and support will stay with me always. Mind you, I am a 34-year-old grown woman who was lost and heart-broken. I remember people telling me that things will get better and thinking, *Ya, right! My whole life has been turned upside down!*

It took about six months before I could drop my daughter off for exchanges without sunglasses to hide my tears. The month after my husband left was chaos. It was only weeks and then he refused to speak to me without using a lawyer. Not only did Shaun want to run away from our marriage but he also wanted everything we ever purchased together—the car, the Crock-Pot my parents gave me for Christmas, the blanket I quilted for our daughter, and, of course, full custody and placement of our daughter.

His family turned their backs to me as well. It was so painful and hard to understand how people who were once loving and support-ive to me could become so mean and cold, and shut me out of their lives. The battle over Leah was one of the hardest struggles I had to face during this awful time. Going to mediation and court was crazy; listening to Shaun talk was surreal. All I could wonder was, *Who is this person and what happened to the loving man that I had married?* What was even more interesting was that he couldn't make eye con-tact and refused to have a conversation with me. All communication had to be done via a co-parenting website.

Looking back over the last two years, thinking about it all still brings me to tears. I know I have become a stronger, braver, more confident person. I feel I have been able to show my now 5-year-old daughter that it is OK to be on your own, you don't need to rely on another person or husband to bring you happiness. Over the last two years, I have slowly put my life back together. We have gotten to this com-fortable place of our Mama-Leah time. Leah has adjusted to our fifty-fifty placement. I was blessed after our long, drawn-out court battle and got school choice that Leah will be attending kindergarten in the town where I now live and had lived prior to my marriage. (My ex-husband had moved also. One year after his surprise departure, he was engaged and is now married.)

Thanks to my parents and brother for supporting me and answering the phone just to have someone listen to me cry and to my co-workers for helping me on days when I felt I spent more time talking with my lawyer then actually working. Thanks to my friend Heather, who always had the best advice and support, responding to e-mail as quickly as I hit the send button. I am so much more humble to people who are divorced (I had never thought I would be one of them).

It takes two people to make a marriage, and if one person gives up then you are left with nothing. When I tell people I'm divorced, they assume I was in a high-conflict marriage and will often say things like, "I'm sure being divorced is better than being with someone you are fighting with all the time." It's often easier to just smile and nod. To try to explain to someone the pain and feelings of abandonment when you have a husband who walks away is something beyond what most people can understand.

I am no longer embarrassed to share with people that I am divorced. After speaking with a counselor over the last two years, I do know that I may not have been a perfect wife (Who is?), but I didn't deserve to be left the way my ex-husband left me. Last week, when I pulled into the T-ball field for my daughter's game, I saw my ex-husband, his new wife, and his parents sitting in the stands. It would have been much easier to just keep driving and skip the game, but I took a deep breath, got out of the car and reminded myself that I have done nothing to be embarrassed of, and tried to confidently sit in the bleachers, smiling and clapping for my beautiful daughter. Shame on them for ignoring me as I smiled and gave them a pretend wave. Life does go on after a runaway husband leaves; this is important to remember when you are in the middle of the nightmare.

58

Suddenly Single

Jane from Cape Town, South Africa
54 years old
Separated seventeen months

I will never forget the day that my husband said he was leaving me. It was January 22, a few weeks after a fun-filled family Christmas, which we had spent at our holiday house that had been built with our retirement in mind only two short years before. He and I had gone for dinner with my family to celebrate my brother's birthday. As we walked into the restaurant, I knew something was bothering him, so while we waited for everyone to arrive, I casually asked if everything was alright. What he said next gave me icy chills.

"I've lost the passion for you. I don't love you anymore and I don't think I can get that back." Straight out, just like that. The room was stifling hot, but I went completely cold and sat there thinking I'd woken up in someone else's nightmare. Strangely, I did not react. I kept it together—no crying or drama.

I was completely and utterly blindsided. There had been no hint of this in our marriage. We were a loving couple who others constantly applauded for being an amazing example to everyone. However, the year before had been an awful year for both of us. His dad had recently died and although they were not close, it affected him deeply. His mother (divorced from his dad for many years) had visited us every year for up to twelve weeks at a time and we were good friends. However, in the past few years, she had become more dominant than ever before and was a force in our life that affected our marriage. My husband could not or would not support me in anything that had to do with his mother, and it took its toll on us, particularly in the last year.

At a New Year's Eve party, I said to him, "Thank goodness this year is over and we can look forward to a brand-new year!" Little did I know that in twenty-three days he would deliver the news that would bring me to my knees. The day after our youngest son turned 21, he moved out, leaving me with his mother, who still had three weeks left of her holiday from the UK. Exactly six months later—to the day—we were divorced.

I was heartbroken to the core. I had never taken my charmed life for granted, always knowing how fortunate I was to have a husband who loved me and I him. I would tell him, "I need you like the air I breathe." We would joke that if we were online dating, we'd be the one the other was looking for. Our friends and family knew our home to be a happy, safe, solid place. We were supposed to grow old together. We were the absolute last couple any of our friends imagined would get a divorce. I truly believed he was my soul mate and my best friend.

And now I was alone, with no explanation as to why he left. It seemed as if this man I'd known and loved for thirty-five years had changed into someone no one recognized. Everyone assumed there was some-one else waiting in the wings to appear so we could all say, "Aha, that's the reason." But to this day, there is no bombshell, no other woman has appeared, and he cannot or will not explain. I Googled "Male midlife crisis" and I am convinced that's exactly what he is going through. He ticks every single box.

I am sad, shocked, and grief stricken. This man who was my rock and my protector is gone. I truly believed that my marriage was forever and that my husband felt the same and wanted to continue to raise our two sons together. Instead I joined the rest of the divorced wives club, where I didn't think I belonged. A mutual friend of ours told my ex-husband that he was making the biggest mistake of his life and that by the time he realized it, I will have moved on. My ex's response? "It's a risk I'm willing to take."

What is so sad for me is that our marriage was good. Even he acknow-ledges this and said to me, "I don't regret a single day of our marriage." We didn't argue or fight (our only real battles were about his mother).

I am still struggling to come to terms with the fact that I had no clue how he felt. I now question everything about our past life together. How long had he been thinking of leaving me? Do I really know this man? What does he really want? Did I miss signs that were there all along?

I understand now that men who suddenly leave their wives are usually conflict avoiders. They don't like to talk about their feelings and will suffer in silence for a long time, and then leave quickly. They very often grew up in a home with a stern, strict, abusive father and so they never learned to deal with conflict—it was far better to walk away and keep quiet than to be punished for daring to argue. They often have an unusually close relationship with their mothers. My ex to a tee.

So where to now? How do I move on and get over this? I consider myself to be strong, independent, and capable of change. In order for me to move on and get over the life-long love of my husband (we'd been together thirty-four years) I needed to understand that the man who left me is a different man to the one I loved and was married to. Otherwise my whole married life was a sham, and I know it wasn't. I need to understand that my husband just didn't want the same relationship anymore and wanted to be free to pursue other women and lead a totally new and different life.

I am very lucky, as I have many different groups of friends and a strong family. They became my human life raft. Every *WhatsApp* message, virtual hug, or coffee date helped drag me up from the quagmire of misery I was sinking into. I kept busy with work, hobbies, sport, and going out. I had no idea of the strength of these women. They still amaze me daily. Through tears and laughter, the validation I got from my friends has helped build my self-esteem back up from the bottom.

As a single woman, I miss having a partner who wanted the best for me, who wouldn't let me fall. I loved that I mattered to someone. But that person failed me. The sadness of what could have been is often all-consuming, but when the pain seems too much to bear, I try to remember that, like grief, it comes in waves. I only have to get through the next one or two hours before it subsides. I also hold on to the belief that there is more than one man I can love in my life and that I am far more than just the wife of the man I was married to. I am learning to love being single, and that it's OK to be alone. I have a freedom I haven't known in over thirty years. I can do anything—it's my life now and I refuse to sink.

59

The Brazilian Taxi Cab Driver's Philosophy of Life

Natalie from Columbus, Ohio, USA
57 years old
Separated five years

It will go down as one of the most difficult and heart-wrenching days in my life. It might seem cliché to say that, but the day still holds a grip on me. The sharpness dulling over time, but it is a memory both my son and I will share for always.

We had just returned to Brazil from the U.S. after hearing from the father of my child that he wanted a divorce. We were vacationing in Ohio with my family at the time, so we needed to return to our home in the southern part of Brazil to deal with this turn of events in both of our lives.

We left the brilliance of summer in Ohio to return to the city of Curitiba, tucked away in the more southern part of the country—not at all the hot, steamy sunlit beach that you may think about when asked to imagine Brazil. It was winter in Curitiba, not a pretty sight. Dark, dreary, chilly, and overcast when my son and I made our way to visit the lawyer, who I hoped would help me find my way out of this muddle.

Even though I am fluent in Portuguese, it doesn't prepare one to take on all the legal details and vocabulary of an international divorce. Then added to that, the emotional turmoil and the need I had to remain strong and confident for my son. Mommy could handle it all, we will solve this impasse and move forward. Compiling the problem was the strong desire my son had to leave Brazil. He knew that leaving the country would limit the opportunities he would have to visit his father, but he had made the choice and I needed to respect his decision. I also felt it would be best to return to the U.S., where I had my support system, my family, so I could better deal with the proceedings.

We had a name of a female lawyer who would be able to help sort through the bureaucracy and prepare the materials we needed to get thorough the divorce. We had scheduled a late-afternoon appointment, and I decided over much internal debate to take my son with me. He hadn't wanted to leave my side since the unanticipated and shocking news from his father. I have to admit I needed him, too.

We took a cab to her office. It was one of those days when you say to yourself that someone is directing this movie—the gloom of the day seemed only to enhance and perhaps exaggerate the heaviness in the air and what we were feeling.

After we arrived, I decided that it would be best for my son to wait in another room while the lawyer and I went through the steps and discussed the materials I needed to prepare. In addition, I thought it was not necessary for my son to hear, once again, the rehashing of the whole event from scene one.

After I had finished a lengthy discussion with the lawyer, my son requested to re-enter the room and express how he was feeling. On one hand, I didn't want him to be intimately involved with this process, but on the other hand, I was so proud of his maturity and ability to truly articulate his feelings on the subject. He told the lawyer that he no longer wanted to remain in Brazil. He loved his father but wanted to return to Ohio and go to school there. His determination and commitment to this only reinforced my own intention to make this happen, and to make it happen as painlessly and as quickly as I could.

The lawyer was energetically mounting her defense—we will trace his funds, we will uncover his hidden assets, we will get the alimony you deserve for twenty-three years of marriage, we will go after him and make him pay. In addition, she wanted me to go and empty out our joint bank account. (A mistake I made, since I didn't do that.) Her desire to help me fight this battle was admirable, and I appreciated her energy and dedication to my cause but I believed she had missed the point that I was trying to make over and over again. Perhaps it was my inability to adequately express myself in Portuguese, but I doubted that; since I had proven to be able handle Portuguese in an academic environment in the past, it wasn't related to my language skills.

I carefully and slowly reiterated my main intention. I said it with all the passion I could muster in this situation while being critically aware of the presence of my son in the room. I wanted two things from this divorce. I wanted to maintain my dignity and I wanted my son.

Those were the two things that meant the most to me. I didn't want revenge, I didn't want his money, and I didn't want him in my life ever again. I wanted to sever the ties, cleanly and correctly. I would make sure that I would be able to provide for my son, while securing his future needs. There was no negotiation for me on these two points. I wanted to leave the country as soon as possible and with my son. That was what we both wanted, and wanted it now. I vowed I would get what I wanted and with my dignity intact.

That was my goal, that was my mission on this cold and dark day. I knew I would win. It would cost me emotionally and take all focus for the next weeks, but I would win. I would win for my son, that was what he wanted.

We left the lawyer's office feeling totally spent. The discussion, the jet lag, the lack of sleep and emotional toll on us hit us like a tidal wave. We called a cab and waited outside in the cold, constant drizzle.

The cab pulled up and we huddled together in the back, letting the dusk that had settled hide our teary eyes. We sat in silence, until the cheerful voice of the cab driver broke into our world. "So you two back there, miserable weather tonight. It has been like this for the last week," called out the driver.

"We wouldn't know," said my son as the words seem to get stuck in his throat, "We just arrived from the States because my father wants to divorce my mom," he continued.

The cab driver quickly became silent and looked in his rearview mirror. He could now see more clearly, the tears rolling down our cheeks. He remained silent for a bit. "Yes," I stated. "That's the reason we are back and why we were at the lawyers office."

He seemed to direct his attention to my son, assuring him that he had a strong mom and things would work out. They began to chatter about cars and places my son had visited. He told us that he had been divorced and had remarried. He was in love with his new wife and had a son with her. But she wanted more money, encouraging him to work long hours and not take time off. He said they had enough money to live, but she wanted more. His love for her and his need to be with his son wasn't enough. She wanted a bigger house, a newer car, and more clothes. She also wanted a divorce. He felt that his love for her wasn't what she really wanted and really needed.

As we neared the house, he became more philosophical in his approach. He could hear the love my son had for his father when he was talking about what he liked to do with him for fun. He heard me say that all this material stuff had no value if your husband and the father of your son didn't want to be with you anymore.

We pulled up the driveway to a huge house, a garage filled with a new and a classic car, a garden that I been lovingly tending for the last years. He stopped talking and turned around to face us in the back seat.

"Your husband, your father has it all. He has a beautiful wife who loved him and his son, a son who wants nothing more than to spend time with him, the house, the cars and garden that grew with love and hope . . . and he decided to throw it all away and for what? He has it all in his hands. I would give my life to have this, have it all, especially the love of a family," he said, choking back his own tears.

He didn't want us to leave. He felt responsible for us. He told us that we could call him if we needed anything—he would take us any-where. He wanted to help. He wanted to give of himself. Maybe he wanted to understand how this could have happened.

I assured him that we were OK and could manage this on our own. I told him I had no answers for how a man, a father could throw his family away in a matter of a few days. But we were strong, we were now a team and will go forward.

A stranger. He reached out his hand and heart. He valued what the father of my child did not. He valued love. He valued family. He valued life.

As I sit here writing this piece, the tears fill my eyes and drip melodically on my bagel. I had told my son that when I write things that move me, I tend to cry and get my bagel all soggy. He said to me, laced with that little sly laugh of his, that the solution was quite simple. He encouraged me to continue writing, he knew how to solve the problem—it was really very obvious. Just buy two bagels.

The simplicity of the solution, the simplicity that exists in life, and the simplicity of the philosophy of the Brazilian taxi driver—the pure and honest simplicity of love.

Postscript:
At the time of the above story, I was vacationing in the U.S. with my 12-year-old son. His father was to arrive on Monday from Brazil, where we had settled. His father is Brazilian. On Friday evening before his arrival, he called me in the U.S., stating that he missed me and couldn't wait to make love.

At 6:00 a.m. Sunday morning, he called, stating he "had a vision" and no longer loved me. He wanted a divorce. He is a highly educated and successful businessman, and we had been married twenty-three years. We were not having marital problems and were in the process of finishing a renovation on a beach property and starting a new renovation on our home. We were seen as an ideal couple by family and friends.

It was a shock—something I never had anticipated. My son was devastated. We returned quickly to Brazil and were divorced in less than three weeks, the speed of which was made possible by his money and influence. I gave in to all demands—I was blackmailed. Basically, I was told that if I wanted to leave the country with my son, I needed to accept the divorce agreement without the assistance of my lawyer.

Five years later, the funds I was promised still remain in Brazil—thousands and thousands of dollars to a U.S. attorney to help me navigate the Brazilian banking and legal system.

Regardless of the struggle to obtain what was stated in the contract, my son and I have moved on. I have reinvented myself—a new career that I love, and my son has a wonderful group of friends and is doing well in school. We have risen from the ashes of a once love affair and beautiful family that had been a team. We are stronger, braver, and more fortunate than I could have imagined.

💔

60

SNAPPED!

Marly from Piermont, New York, USA
60 years old
Separated four years

After receiving a request to connect with another writer/editor on a well-known professional online networking site, I hit the Accept button, which routed me to a roster of more potential connections and, hopefully, opportunities. Second row down, I spotted a familiar name (sans photograph) and clicked on the link that brought me to the man's home page. Once there, I scrolled through the bio and quickly realized this was the same Carl Franks I met in Los Angeles years ago, before I was married. But ours wasn't a business relationship. Carl was the first man who ever spanked me—recreationally.

At first we were like old friends reuniting, each of us spinning out the details of the recent past. But then our Internet/phone-based relationship took an unexpected turn and, within a month and a half, my new "old friend" became my long-distance disciplinarian (dom) and I his submissive (sub). My husband and mate of almost two decades knew nothing about this liaison, but I swept aside any misgivings, rationalizing that what I was doing was a good thing, as it got me back in touch with my sexuality. Oddly, I was able to take the excitement I felt playing this "game" back to the bedroom, helping to rectify my troubled love life at home, which had always been an issue due to my lack of physical desire for my husband, who really was my best friend and strongest advocate.

But day by day, like the quintessential drug addict, I wanted more, and my cravings and obsession with BDSM escalated to the point where I was desperate to go beyond the online playground. I needed a real-life experience. So, at the suggestion of my long-distance dom, I contacted a New York City–based disciplinarian of the female persuasion—a move designed to alleviate the guilt I knew I'd feel if I solicited a man to indulge me. I even told my husband what I was planning, and he actually gave me his blessing. "Whatever it takes," he'd said. He even seemed a bit turned on by the idea. (I was elated!)

However, I soon developed an unhealthy emotional dependence on my disciplinarian, which I eventually tried to break by connecting with another male dominant in "the scene." And this was after I drove hundreds of miles to "play" with my dom, something I simply had to do. In retrospect this was probably the biggest mistake I made, as I'm sure my husband sensed something, since I was often glued to my phone, waiting for incoming texts. But at the time, this did not seem to be a big deal, as I had no intention of leaving my marriage and I was certainly not in love with this man. I also knew, unequivocally, that my husband would never leave me; he, after all, adored me—an observation made by many of my friends.

In all honesty (or perhaps in my delusional state), life seemed pretty darn good. My husband and I still loved each other's company and certainly, the sex was better than ever. We were also enjoying rehabbing our recently purchased summer home in New England, a 180-year-old Victorian overlooking one of the most beautiful lakes on the planet. In fact, often on our walks down the hill into the small, cozy village, I would remark how lucky we were and how content I felt.

But the laws of physics being what they are (for every action there is an equal and opposite reaction), life as I once knew it was suddenly over. I found out my husband had slept with a friend of mine, and he wasn't going to stop. He also wasn't coming back to New York, where I had just returned for some appointments; he was going to stay up north. And this was just four days after he'd told me how I had helped him grow and how good we were for each other—and, yes, that he was still in love with me. But as he stated, "it was his turn now," since he'd always been married and never had the freedom of being single, as I did during my 20s and 30s. (This was not his first marriage.) But that, at least, was not my fault. He also made it clear that there was no point in doing therapy. "Why bother?" he'd said.

I then found myself on a wild, emotional rollercoaster ride over the next seven months as I tried to figure out why I had chosen to throw myself down this rabbit hole. I began looking for answers (on the Internet, through my talks with close friends, my family, and therapist) while frantically searching for ways to cope with a tremendous sense of abandonment and post-traumatic stress, waking up every morning feeling as if I was being electrocuted. After all, not only did I lose my life partner overnight; I also happened to lose my income stream and was faced with the potential loss of the roof over my head and my beloved cat, who was nearing the end of her time on earth.

I grappled with bouts of grief, rage, and extreme melancholy, bumbling my way through alcohol-fueled nights and Xanax-filled mornings, often times railing at a God, who I was not sure I believed in. I pleaded with my husband, writing e-mails late at night, listing in insane detail what a wonderful marriage we had and how much we had in common. I even consulted with psychics, wanting to know if he'd ever come back.

With perverse fascination, I watched as the world around me began to uncannily reflect my internal landscape, including the time I found the hallway covered with maggots that had apparently come in through the wheat-based kitty litter. And then there was the destruction of half the backyard due to a microburst that appeared out of nowhere, and the electrical fire next door after a freak snowstorm in October downed power lines. As a friend of mine said, it was, indeed, an unrelenting "shit storm."

Desperate for distractions, I also opened myself up to situations that would likely have never occurred under normal circumstances—including a protracted dalliance with a 25-year-old Orthodox Jewish man that culminated in a very awkward, pathetically funny, one-night fling, made even more humorous by the fact that I am a total shiksa and old enough to be his mother.

It was a game-changing chapter of my life that I will never, ever forget. But, all told, I learned some valuable lessons about love, relationships, and spirituality—while gaining a deeper understanding of "self."

Whew, what a trip it was. But I've managed to move on (and even wrote a book about it) and am now in a relationship with a wonderful man with whom I feel deeply connected on all levels—emotional, spiritual, physical. But that's not to say I'm totally healed. It takes time, and sudden spousal abandonment is different than it is when couples make the decision to separate or divorce after years of fighting and struggle. And no one knows this better than Vikki Stark.

61

Making Ice Cream to Heal a Broken Heart

Emma from Wimbledon, England, UK
47 years old
Separated two years

My story goes back to the summer of 2014. I am two years along from the day he announced over dinner in a restaurant and completely out of the blue that he had outgrown me, was bored of me, uninspired by day-to-day family life, and felt he could find a better wife who would make him feel more loved and cherished. He said he had fifty years left of his life and he wanted to enjoy it and feel true happiness. He went on to say that after months of consideration, he felt that although I was, in his opinion, a fantastic mother, I had not been a good-enough wife and had failed my duties. He said that I only had myself to blame that he had to leave.

He had also been writing a list of my failings, which he read out to me over the course of the next few weeks, a list that he had been compiling for months. He could see that I was bewildered, crushed, and devastated, but he just kept on saying horrible things. He was unable to show any compassion to me. I still run those words through my head and really need to stop replaying them. They serve no positive purpose but somehow comfort me in knowing what a load of nonsense his reasons were when he walked away.

After twenty-seven years together (twenty-three married) and three fabulous sons (now aged 11, 15 and 18), I know the truth. It always comes out in the end. The truth being he had met someone new. What an embarrassing cliché. Added to the fact he had bought a

Ferrari, started doing endless triathlons, and been buying young trendy clothes, listening to rap music, going clubbing, and basically having a midlife crisis at the age of 47. At the time he was saying all of the cruel things he said to me, I believed every word, but now I see they were just ridiculous reasons to justify his walking away.

I begged him not to break up our family. I said I would do anything to save our marriage and family. He said it was too late, which I could not understand. He is quite simply a cowardly, dishonourable, and selfish man. He has never taken responsibility or apologised for what he did to us. He has just lied and hurt us for two years. Our lives changed course in 2014, and it has taken up until this point (and I know further) to truly recover from the crushing and heartless blow he dealt us. We did not deserve it.

He decided to leave and never had the decency to let me fight for our marriage or family, my greatest life's work. He made the decision to leave on his own and made this decision many months before he decided to tell me. He made a decision that would affect four other lives without bothering to have a conversation with me. He dismissed my feelings and treated me with no love or respect. He looked at me and delivered the news like I was a stranger and spoke to me like I was his enemy. We had been best friends for thirty years, and now he just wanted out as fast as he could.

He turned from a loving husband and father into a cold, removed, and cruel man overnight. He could not get away from us quick enough. He was in a great hurry to flee his responsibilities and move on very quickly with his new-found "happy" life. He rewrote twenty-seven years of history by saying that "looking back he does not think we was ever really happy and had ever felt loved enough." It's laughable, terribly painful, completely insulting, and utterly ridiculous. I still feel like I lived a lie and wonder if he ever meant the kind things he said me in the past. He would say, "You are my heart" to me regularly for years and years. He wrote it on everything.

My youngest son and I decided to find a hobby that would distract us from the shock, sadness, and abandonment that we were living through, so we decided we would master the art of ice cream making to heal our broken hearts. This hobby helped us through the sad and dreadful months that we had to wade through after he left. Stracciatella ice cream with chocolate chunks became our specialty! My other sons helped us eat it. We all found comfort in the simple day-to-day things at home that made us feel secure at a time when our world had been turned upside down.

Two years along and we still make ice cream every week and enjoy sitting together watching our favourite TV shows, playing cards, and eating our homemade ice cream each night. Approximately 730 nights later and our ice cream ritual is still going strong and so are we. We no longer make ice cream to distract us from how sad, devastated, hurt, confused, and shocked we are or how we could not come to terms with how badly we have been treated by the person we loved so much, the person who should have shielded his sons and me from hurt and pain, who hurt us more than anyone ever had.

Now we make ice cream because it's our thing, our very special thing, it's delicious and we love it!!! Our ice cream hobby helped us heal and recover, along with the endless love, comfort, and support of the most loving family and friends anyone could ask for. Lucky us!

One day we will make a batch of ice cream for you, Vikki!

62

Women Stand Together in Strength

Alison from Gorey, Ireland
48 years old
Separated five years ago

It all began just after the bad snow here in Ireland in the winter of 2010. He had moved away to the U.K. to work and was staying with his parents' 70-year-old friends. They had one daughter, who had two sons from two different marriages. I never suspected anything until he came home on March 5, 2011, and said, "I don't love you anymore." He had just the week before had a vasectomy much to my disbelief. Why would he do that when he's living away? Still I did not suspect.

I had just collected him from the airport as he'd returned for a visit. I gripped the steering wheel when I heard those words "I don't love you," feeling numb as his words resonated through my brain. It took me till the August to admit it was happening. He phoned the girls and told them on loudspeaker. I was in complete denial. I went down to eight stone. I was absolutely paralysed for I would say three years. I could only accept the support that came to my doorstep; I lost friends along the way. I was incapable of communicating with anyone. To this day, I can only think the reason he left was that he was unable to relate to the older girls who were actually more mature than he was.

Since he left, he has fallen back to where I met him as a teenager, drinking in the pub, no responsibility, tattoos, holidays away. Looking back, he never grew up. I see that I married a man who was broken; his father left him at 18 and he never dealt with it. My brother was killed at that time; we were both broken. I always told him how to behave, what to wear, he was always instigating and never could be told what to do. He was from a completely different background from me. I did love him at one stage, of course, and we had three beautiful girls.

How did I survive this? I went for weekly counselling. I have a few very close friends who had also separated. This was my saving grace. My faith in God has brought me full circle; during my suicidal moments it was my belief that got me through. I could not have done this alone. I have become a much stronger person out of this. I adore my girls and they adore me. I don't see him, speak to him—communication is by e-mail only. He does not want to engage. I never thought I'd come out of this depression and the cycle I found myself in until I was ready to make that step to recovery, to want to heal. I felt worthless. Having read *Runaway Husbands*, I realised other people felt the same as I did and the betrayal they felt meant I wasn't alone.

To you women out there: remember that we are strong women, but you will only recover if it is what you want, to want to live a life fulfilled. I will never let him destroy my life. I will show my ex that I am a strong woman. I now feel after all this time that I have thawed out and want to live again. It can only happen though if you consciously want to live on, alive and confident in whom you are. It does get easier. I do still have my down days, my days of feeling sorry for myself. When that comes, I have to make a choice to stay with the feeling or fight it. Let us women stand together in strength. We can and we will move on!

I hope this helps whoever reads this.

Join the Community of
Women Helping Women

Please visit www.RunawayHusbands.com
to connect with other women who
have also experienced
Wife Abandonment Syndrome.

You will learn about resources, events and
retreats to help you in your healing.

Our community is there for you!

www.RunawayHusbands.com